SERVING TO LEAD

SERVING to LEAD

Lieutenant General
Sir Freddie Viggers
KCB CMG MBE DL

Copyright © 2018 Lieutenant General Sir Freddie Viggers
KCB CMG MBE DL

The moral right of the author has been asserted.

Apart from any fair dealing for the purposes of research or private study, or criticism or review, as permitted under the Copyright, Designs and Patents Act 1988, this publication may only be reproduced, stored or transmitted, in any form or by any means, with the prior permission in writing of the publishers, or in the case of reprographic reproduction in accordance with the terms of licences issued by the Copyright Licensing Agency. Enquiries concerning reproduction outside those terms should be sent to the publishers.

Matador
9 Priory Business Park,
Wistow Road, Kibworth Beauchamp,
Leicestershire. LE8 0RX
Tel: 0116 279 2299
Email: books@troubador.co.uk
Web: www.troubador.co.uk/matador
Twitter: @matadorbooks

ISBN 978 1789014 983

British Library Cataloguing in Publication Data.
A catalogue record for this book is available from the British Library.

Printed and bound in the UK by TJ International, Padstow, Cornwall
Typeset in 11pt Minion Pro by Troubador Publishing Ltd, Leicester, UK

Matador is an imprint of Troubador Publishing Ltd

These memoirs are dedicated to the men and women of the British Army, their families and our friends, who have given me such a rewarding and fulfilling career in my life. I owe them.

But mainly, this is for Jane and our children.

CONTENTS

Acknowledgements	ix
Introduction	xi
Foreword by General the Lord Dannatt	xiii
A Very Close Run Thing	xvii

LEARNING TO LEAD

Paddock to Parade Ground	3
Leaps and Bounds	13
First tour	22
Early lessons in leadership: Bramcote and J (Sidi Rezegh) Battery, Royal Horse Artillery	42
Introducing Harry	55
Back to school	63
Germany, Canada, Northern Lights: Revisited	70
First Infantry Brigade	79
Staff College and the Brighton Bomb: Protecting the Margarets	86

SERVE TO LEAD

Best job (so far)	107
Back to the MOD	117
Bosnia (first time)	125
A new strategy for people	141
Bosnia (revisited)	147
Jacko	160
Iraq & the Inquiry	169
Military Secretary & Adjutant General	181
Black Rod	202

THE ROAD BACK

Medical Journey	229
Brown Rod	240
So What?	246
Appendix 1 – CV	259
Appendix 2 – Iraq Inquiry	263

ACKNOWLEDGEMENTS

First, I must thank and acknowledge the example and lessons I have learned from my Army commanders and leaders, especially Lords Bramall and Walker and Generals Sir Mike Jackson and Sir Rupert Smith. Next, our daughter, Kate, has shown her boundless enthusiasm as my editor. Her eye for detail, critical application and efficiency deserves a medal. I am very grateful to Lord Dannatt for writing the Foreword to this book. He was an excellent supporter to me before I retired as Adjutant General.

Likewise, John Pitt Brooke CB has been a great friend to me. John is a retired civil servant whom I first met in the Ministry of Defence and he worked with me in my last tour before retirement. Now, as the Chief Executive of the Armed Forces Pension Society, he has been a source of reassurance, support and encouragement. Most recently, I have become involved with Jim Davidson. Jim is absolutely devoted to the military and has been involved with many charities, as well as continuing to entertain the troops on operational duty. Jim's latest venture is Care after Combat and I pay tribute to him and his great charity later. Felicity and Tori deserve special thanks for their help and advice as commentators on the early draft of my book. The story has changed quite a bit since I first started writing it. My publishers Troubador have been commendably helpful and understanding throughout the project. Nothing has been too much trouble and I am delighted with the result.

My wife, Jane, appears throughout this. She has lived and seen most of it, and her love, friendship and sheer determination have kept my spirits up when I needed it. She's a great lady.

Finally, I thank my son, Brendan; his wife, Becky; my daughter, Kate; her husband, Jay; and all their children for their love and support. Living for them has become incredibly important for me now. Equally, my sister, Carolyn; godparents, Margaret Fry and her brother, Reed Dawe; my cousins and their families have meant much too. They're a good tribe to belong to.

INTRODUCTION

Black Rod, the job I was doing and loved, came to a sudden end in May 2010. The stroke has done lasting but tolerable damage, not the least of which is memory loss. So as I was recovering, Jane, my wonderful wife, best friend and carer, said that I should commit my memories to paper before I lose them altogether and, if only for the benefit of others, so that someday our grandchildren can learn about who I was before I became their 'Franpa'. After my stroke, motivation has not been my strongest point but, increasingly, more and more of my friends have said the same thing: "you should write a book." There appears to be a willing and eager readership keen to hear about my Service career and experiences in Parliament. Now, with the help of my daughter, Kate, as scribe - and with plenty of time on my hands - I really have no excuses left. Writing the book has been an unexpectedly helpful exercise – a kind of therapy; recounting that life-changing moment in 2010, what led up to that point and what has occurred since, has helped me come to terms with all that has happened.

Publishing these memoirs is also timely as it marks ten years since my retirement from the Army and coincides with my recent role as President of the veterans' charity Care After

Combat, set up by Jim Davidson OBE in 2014. The penultimate chapter explains more about that role and the charity, and it is my intention that whatever proceeds are made from this book will go towards funding that valuable work.

So, I will tell my story and share the lessons I have learned along the way, for the benefit of my family and the many friends who might be interested. The opinions are mine, along with any mistakes in the retelling (blame the stroke). I hope that those who served with me along the way will look back on my account, covering the last forty years or so of my military life and what followed, and will enjoy the tale and the memories it creates.

I am aware that I could have included lots of names of people who have influenced my story. These will be known and mean something to those who have served with me but are likely to have little relevance to a wider readership. In the interests of brevity, I have therefore omitted the many who deserve a mention. They know who they are and I hope they will understand.

Finally, I have used photographs from my own collection and those given to me to illustrate each section. In particular Deryc Sands, the official photographer in the House of Lords and a real expert on Historical and Ceremonial occasions, was kind enough to let me use images from his collection, including the front cover.

FOREWORD BY
GENERAL THE LORD DANNATT
GCB, CBE, MC, DL

Just before I began to exercise the privilege of writing this Foreword to Lieutenant General Sir Freddie Viggers' inspirational memoir "Serving to Lead", I had the pleasure of seeing Freddie and his wife, Jane, again in London. They were in Black Rod's office, surrounded by his former staff, and about to have lunch with Sarah Clarke, the first ever Lady Usher of the Black Rod. It was typical of the camaraderie of the House of Lords for Sarah to invite Freddie back to the Palace of Westminster, and to the office where his illustrious career had reached its climax but where he nearly lost his life. And the Freddie I saw on Thursday 19th July 2018 looked larger than life itself, cracking jokes as always and with Jane, as ever by his side. This very special memoir tells the story of Lieutenant General Sir Freddie Viggers – a soldier at heart, and a fighter to the core.

There is no doubt that the near fatal stroke that Freddie suffered in the early hours of Tuesday 18th May 2010 changed the course of Freddie and Jane's life dramatically. However, the way that Freddie has responded to this sudden change in his circumstances is entirely consistent with everything that he achieved during his career. This memoir charts his remarkable progression from school, to Sandhurst, to one of the highest ranks in the British Army, to hold one of the most historic appointments in the land and on to being a much-loved husband, father and grandfather – or "Franpa" as his grandchildren call him.

Freddie's choice of title for his book – "Serving to Lead" – captures what is best about the British Army and about one of the most popular and successful generals in modern times. The motto of the Royal Military Academy Sandhurst – "Serve to Lead" – is a notion on which all Officer Cadets are required to ponder during their training but probably only fully understand as experiences grow. The heart of the British Army is its people, the backbone of the British Army is its Warrant Officers and

Sergeants but as an organisation it is only really successful when its Commissioned Officers exercise inspirational leadership implementing well thought through plans and drawing the best out of the soldiers alongside whom they have the privilege to serve. This selfless commitment, which is one of the Army's six core values, has been the hallmark of Freddie Viggers' career. This memoir chronicles Freddie's active service on operations in Northern Ireland, Bosnia and Iraq, underpinned by his love for his regiment, 3rd Regiment Royal Horse Artillery.

With people very much in the forefront of his professional mind, it was perhaps inevitable that Sir Freddie Viggers' military career would culminate in his appointment as the Adjutant General, the Army's most senior personnel officer. He filled that appointment between 2005 and 2008 at a time when the British Army was under its greatest pressure since the Second World War. Intense operations in Iraq and Afghanistan were placing inordinate demands on soldiers and families alike. Freddie championed the Military Covenant working on issues such as pay, accommodation and welfare provision to try to restore some balance between the unlimited operational liability expected of soldiers and the necessary individual support that they have a right to expect. One of Freddie's greatest disappointments, and mine too, was when the Government of the day turned down his well-intentioned proposal for there to be a Veterans Commissioner. Had that proposal been accepted then Freddie would have been an ideal first incumbent. But it was not to be, thereby offering the possibility for Freddie to follow the alternative opportunity of applying to become the Gentleman Usher of the Black Rod, an appointment that he clearly loved and in which he thrived, succeeding beyond measure.

Freddie's appointment as Black Rod brought together all the main themes of his professional career. The close association of Black Rod to the Queen was a logical extension of nearly four decades of service to Her Majesty in the British Army. Having fought the Queen's enemies on many battlefields, it was entirely appropriate to take up a role in Parliament where the key decisions are taken deciding the future of the Armed Forces, and their employment. The role of Black Rod, by its very nature, was demanding; yet it enabled more time to be with Jane, the children and grandchildren. This was something always in short supply while he was serving in the Army. Commitment to people – his family and his soldiers – has always been one of Freddie's key drivers. Even after his illness and significant recovery he went on to work with Jim Davidson as President of Care after Combat. If anyone needed care after combatting a major life challenge, it was Freddie. Thus, it was entirely typical of this remarkable man that he would go on giving to others, and still does.

I warmly commend this book to those who know and love Freddie, to those who have served with him and also to the general reader who wants an insight into the career of a truly outstanding British soldier and citizen. The openness and honesty of this account, in the good times and the challenging ones, gives it an authenticity that is compelling. This is indeed a tremendous account of someone who really understands the realities of serving others in order to have the privilege of leading them – "Serving to Lead".

Richard Dannatt
Keswick, Norfolk

A VERY CLOSE RUN THING

5am, Tuesday, 18 May, 2010. The House of Lords Rehearsal Group was gathered at the Sovereign's Entrance, awaiting my arrival to oversee the final walk-through for the State Opening of Parliament. The dress rehearsal for the ceremony always takes place in the early hours, when Whitehall is closed and Parliament is quiet, to ensure safe passage for the Sovereign's escort and the mounted cavalry, and to allow enough time to clear up after the horses. The weeks leading up to this occasion are understandably pressured; there are fixtures and fittings for about 2,000 spectators to place, personnel to brief, security measures to implement and triple check, all according to strict protocol.

Before the ceremony, as part of the rehearsal, I was required to accompany the Lord Great Chamberlain, the Marquess of Cholmondley, in his role as the Queen's escort on a walk-through of the processional route, including the Grand Staircase, The Queen's Robing Room, The Royal Gallery and The Lords' Chamber. In addition to planning and leading the work before the event, my job as Black Rod was to iron out any last-minute issues and to demonstrate that everything had been suitably arranged ahead of Her Majesty's impending arrival.

My team was expecting me at 04:30.

I didn't arrive.

Punctuality has been a lifelong compulsion, born from my Sandhurst training; friends and family will testify to the fact that I hate to be late. For anything. I'm not sure what my team suspected at the time but they were worried for me. Perhaps a missed my alarm and I had slept in; I was never a particularly heavy drinker, so surely not a hangover?

The horses and escorts arrived, of course, precisely at the appointed hour and they all had to carry on without me. When the rehearsal was over, my concerned deputy, Ted Lloyd Jukes, accompanied by Bill Mott, the Garrison Sergeant Major of London district, used a spare key to access my flat, across the road from Westminster Palace. They found me in the bedroom. I had suffered a massive stroke.

Much earlier that morning, I had in fact woken in good time and the day had begun like any other; a coffee, a smoke and BBC Radio. But sitting at the kitchen table, I felt strange and dizzy. There was still time before I needed to report to the House. I went back to the bedroom for a quick lie down.

The next thing I remember is voices, reassuring me that an ambulance was on the way. I couldn't move. Then, blue lights. Then, nothing.

I came round in the Intensive Care Unit (ICU) two days later at King's Hospital and saw my wife, Jane, standing over me. I had an indescribable thirst and there were tubes everywhere. I don't remember anybody explaining to me that I'd had a stroke (although I'm assured that they did, numerous times – perhaps wilful forgetfulness on my part). I do remember there were concerns about mobility, kidney function, my heart. My prognosis was bleak. The stroke had been caused by a dissected aorta, which in turn had led to a catastrophic surge of blood to the brain.

I later learned all the grisly details.

On the afternoon of the stroke, my children, Brendan and Kate, had arrived at the hospital to meet Jane; apparently I recognised them but I was in too much discomfort to communicate. The family kept vigil while decisions were made. The swelling to my brain caused by the blood loss required emergency cranial surgery to remove part of my skull, which would relieve the excruciating pressure and give the brain ("what brain?" friends will ask) room to expand. Doctors advised Jane not to go through with this operation because they could not guarantee a quality of life. But if they didn't operate? Game over. Jane knew my feelings. To live my life from the (relatively) young age of fifty-eight in a wheelchair, dependent on care, unable to enjoy my family, friends and pursuits, would for me be a kind of 'living death'. But she also felt strongly that, unless the medical team could say with 100% certainty that I would end up in a vegetative state, there was still a chance and I deserved to take it. Lucky for me.

Jane tells me that, as they wheeled me away for the first operation, I squeezed her hand and said, "We're going to crack this." My first and only lucid comment. I have no memory of that but I think it helped Jane enormously to feel she was making the right choice. 'Her Freddie' was still there.

Following that initial surgery, I remained in isolation in the ICU for ten days. There were further operations. Open heart surgery repaired the damaged aortal valve but vital organ functions had been compromised; when I was whisked back into theatre with internal bleeding, the ICU nurses told Jane they didn't expect to see me back on the ward again.

I did come back. In a lot of pain and confusion. And it took me a long time to appreciate the impact of what had happened to me.

For many days following my transfer across town from King's College Hospital to St Thomas' Hospital, where I remained for six weeks before moving on to the National Neurological Hospital (NNH), I was convinced that I was holed up somewhere in the Lords, late for a meeting. My family patiently responded to my incessant requests for time checks and my repeated nagging about appointments I was failing to keep.

A nurse asked Jane, "Does he often hallucinate? He says he's supposed to be having lunch with the Queen!"

"Actually," Jane replied, "he is."

Ironically, the stroke resulted in some immediate health improvements. Giving up smoking for one. In the early days, Kate gently declined the repeated 'missions' I gave her to "fetch my pack of fags." I was given a stern talking to by a consultant on that score, although it was the mention of giving up driving, not smoking, that really hit home.

And, in fact, it wasn't the fags that had directly caused the stroke (the surgeons said when they opened my chest up, they'd rarely seen such a healthy pair of smoker's lungs), though I'm sure the forty-three-year habit didn't help. The real culprit – my heart defect – was first picked up in an Army medical in the mid-70s. I'd been subjected to regular health checks from then onwards. In the 80s, I was told that heart surgery would be required one day.

Then there followed a series of jobs that were bloody hard work – demanding and often relentless schedules, full diaries, commitments, a lot of thinking, pressure and expectation, long hours, travel. I enjoyed every one of them; I was an unreformed workaholic. The final three years from 2005-2008 as Adjutant General were incredibly intense – a real grind – and, by the time I retired from the Army, I was tired. When you've operated at a certain level of activity, you know you can sustain it for a defined period of time because there's an end point. It's not until you get to that end point and you switch off that you realise how knackered you are. I wasn't fit, I'd put on a bit of weight which the golf wasn't shifting. Retirement offered a chance for long-term, healing R&R.

But then… I was headhunted for the Black Rod job by my predecessor in the role. I was selected and I plugged straight back in. It was just as busy and complicated as any job I'd held, though in some ways easier thanks to an excellent team and clearly defined objectives. I loved it. In many ways, everything I had done and achieved in my Service Career had been a preparation for my role in Parliament. I had seen and done things that gave me invaluable pointers and experiences, watched and learned some good and bad lessons from those around me, taken risks and survived. Parliament gave me the opportunity to put these lifetime lessons and values into practice.

So there I was, a year into the Black Rod job and I hadn't had a health check-up in years; life had got in the way. Some internal alarm sent me to the House of Lords medical team, just a few days before my personal D-Day, to get checked out. I was diagnosed as having a low risk of a stroke. *Crack on*, I thought. The very next week – a medical crisis that would change my life forever.

Jane says that it was during my long stay at NNH, where I was given daily neuro and physical exercises to perform, that my limitations started to become painfully obvious. I began to register what my debilitated condition meant for my career. The Peers and my bosses at the House of Lords were incredibly understanding and patient, and I'll always be grateful for the time and space they gave me, but finding a way back was going to be harder than I'd imagined. I sensed that I had failed the Queen, the woman to whom I had been loyal for thirty-six years as an Army Officer (although when I was invited to a farewell audience with Her Majesty, she could not have been kinder). Loyalty to a person or cause is for me an essential quality.

In my time as an Army Officer, the Queen has featured large in my life. She was the person whose health and life I toasted as my Captain General at the end of each Regimental occasion; whom I hosted on formal visits; I attended private lunch parties and, later, met her on a personal basis. I met most members of the Royal Family too. All of them have come to represent something that I hold to be important and would have gone as far as to say necessary to protect and preserve. Giving my life in the Army to the Sovereign is, for me, a worthwhile calling and I am proud to have given her my loyalty. I struggle to have sympathy with those who do not do the same, or even question the need for a monarchy or other organisation. The lessons of history have been lost. In any given profession or walk of life, I believe that loyalty has to be assured or cohesion fails. Respect, on the other hand, has to be earned.

In the end, when it came to my health, conversations with an old boss, General Sir Mike Jackson (known to us all as 'Jacko'), helped me come to terms with life as we now knew it and the reality of stepping down as Black Rod.

I had come to know Jacko well and respected him completely. We worked together closely for a number of years, in Bosnia, in Wilton, when he was Commander in Chief, and in the Ministry of Defence in London, when he became Chief of the General Staff, the Head of the Army, at what was an extremely busy time. His excellent autobiography *Soldier* tells the story. He was an exceptional commander in a variety of roles and I came to enjoy and trust his leadership, experience, judgement, and his ability to pick up on the 'big idea'. He also had a very good sense of humour and was always direct and straightforward. He and his wife, Sarah, were good friends to us both and I knew that I could go to him when I needed help and an honest opinion; that he would not let me down. He looked after me in many ways. He said I could not return and do the job properly.

During my stay in hospital, I thought constantly about my future. One evening, I was taken out for supper by the Parliamentary Security Co-ordinator. We had worked on the Security Plan for the Palace of Westminster. I knew I could trust his opinion, too. I asked him for his honest view of what I should do about my stroke and the future. He had seen quite a lot of me during my recovery and his opinion was very clear; he did not think I could deliver what was expected of me (including visits to Westminster Hall by the Pope, Her Majesty the Queen and President Obama in the coming six months) and that I should retire. This was not what I wanted to hear but I knew he and Jacko were telling the truth. The game was up.

It was a disaster for me and the hardest decision I have ever had to take.

LEARNING TO LEAD

PADDOCK TO PARADE GROUND

By the time I retired from the Army in 2008, I had completed thirty-six years' active Service – but the only scar I bore was that given to me by Sally, a bad-tempered Dartmoor pony, at the age of four.

Sally was a birthday present from my Grandfather, delivered by him to Honey Tor Farm at Gulworthy, near Tavistock, where I grew up and we lived with my parents and Grandfather and Grandmother, Caroline. I was allowed to ride Sally to school and back, until we came to blows and she kicked me in the face (jeopardising my eyesight and leaving a scar above my eye socket). Up until then, it had been the most enjoyable commute of my life.

I was born in Yelverton, close to Plymouth, in June 1951. My mother, Ruth Elizabeth Dawe, came from a family of three and her brother and sister, Reed and Margaret, became my godparents. The late Dame Margaret Fry and her brother both had a farming background and they grew up in a culture of getting on with the job without complaining, a national quality and attitude that came from the time of WW2. Uncle Reed farmed at Southcoombe at Milton Abbot near Tavistock, a 200-acre place that formed part of the Duke of Bedford's estate and was bordered by the River Tamar.

Reed's daughter, Liz, explains that his South Devon herd of some forty cows were hand milked and it required a very early start to get the milk churns to the pick-up point on time. My duty on holidays was to collect the cows from the fields in the afternoon and to count and check the hundred sheep, usually by pony. Most of the rest of the farm was devoted to cultivating hay, barley and oats, together with several tons of vegetables, including potatoes, turnips and cabbages. A couple of carthorses were used to plough and harvest the land and they grazed in the orchard close to the farmhouse. Apples would produce fifty-six gallons of cider every year and I was often sent to collect a jug for lunch from the dark cellar. The house and cellar below felt very large to me. Cider was a dangerous brew, particularly on a hot summer's day, and I was not allowed to drink too much.

Aunt Margaret's story is quite similar to Reed's. Her husband, John Fry, grew up at Emsworthy and his father bought Thorne Farm near Lifton, some two miles away, as their wedding present. Together, they comprised about 350 acres. John eventually farmed both places as a single entity. When I was five, my family, now joined by my little sister, Carolyn, moved away to Wellington, Somerset. I missed farm life but school holidays were spent on one or other of the farms owned by the family. Reed took Sally in. He and Vera had three children – Liz, Graham and Nick.

When I stayed with the family, I enjoyed the discipline of early rising to help with the milking, or days involving hay harvest, sheep counting and catching, cow fetching, and reacquainting myself with Sally for rides down to the Tamar to play at fishing and stone-skimming. On the farm, my godparents Reed and Margaret taught me the importance of being reliable, respecting the livestock I was handling, and avoiding injuring myself on the farm's heavy equipment. One look from them was all that needed to be said.

The Frys had three boys, my cousins. Jeremy provided this history of Thorne. Patrick would eventually take on Emsworthy and joined in with the milking herd at Thorne, which would eventually be handed down to the youngest brother, Robert. Sheep, cattle, corn, hay and silage were grown to feed their herds of cows, cattle and sheep. At weekends, we went off to watch John play for Launceston rugby club. During the game, Margaret prepared the post-match refreshments, leaving me to play touch rugby with the other children. That is how I discovered my love for the game and was later able to play at junior level for the club whenever I could. I have always admired the older players for looking after me and later watched the progress of the Launceston All Blacks (called "Laansun" by the Cornish) with interest. They never did quite as well as their Kiwi namesakes, although Cornish players did have some success at County Championship level.

John and Margaret had a large group of friends and I remember a busy social life as Margaret became more involved in fundraising for her local hospital and in politics. Meanwhile, his rugby playing days over, John took up his interest in motor racing and hosting shooting parties. John used The Arundel Arms Hotel in Lifton as his operating base and I can remember going there a lot as a lad.

It was an idyllic childhood – straight from the pages of a boy's adventure story. Small wonder the Army would eventually hold such appeal. It is interesting to think that, in my lifetime, farming has progressed from hand milking to robotics, where the whole operation can be controlled, monitored and repaired on the farm by a laptop virtually from anywhere in the world, and from carthorses for ploughing and harvesting to using hi-tech equipment and other heavy rural machinery. The scale and pace of change in the farming industry has been extraordinary.

After attending junior and middle school, I joined the ranks of 200 boys at the independent Wellington School. Our home at Shuteleigh in Wellington was just a short walk to school and my journey was to become a reminder of the story of Arthur Wellesley, the renowned Duke of Wellington. The Iron Duke was best known for his many successful campaigns against Napoleon in the Peninsula War in Spain and, most famously, the Battle of Waterloo in Belgium in June 1815. The Battle is commemorated by the Wellington Monument. Begun in 1817 and completed in 1854, it is a 175-foot high triangular obelisk that dominates the valley south of the town at a high point on the Blackdown Hills. Designed to represent the bayonet used by the soldiers in the Battle, it was certainly a hi-tech weapon of its time. The Monument is a short detour off the M5 Motorway towards Exeter and offers a stunning and highly recommended view. Much later on, I had no idea that the Duke would feature in my life again.

From the day I arrived, I was taught French by David Elkington, a remarkable teacher who nurtured in me a talent for speaking languages. This would be excellent preparation for later life; grappling with German at Sandhurst and, later, on overseas postings; enjoying and practising French during family holidays and a stint working with the Foreign Legion in Bosnia in 1995. Other subject reports were mixed. Geography: "He has small chance of success." True; I got lost on the way to my Commissioning Ball at the Hurlingham in London after 'passing out' of Sandhurst.

In 1966, Margaret Fry asked me to become Godfather to Robert and we travelled to their farm for the Christening service at Broadwood, close to the Fry's family home. The timing of the service was unfortunate as it was to take place on the same day as England played Germany at Wembley in the final of the football World Cup. We clearly had to get Rob christened and return home in time to watch the game. Aware of his task, the vicar galloped through the service and we raced home, getting back just in time to watch the victory for England that is now so familiar and has been seen by millions worldwide. It has always been easy to remember Godson Rob's birthday since that time (although I've been a bit lax at marking it; sorry, Rob).

That same year, my parents' separation would impact life for us all and, with hindsight, I guess I saw it coming. There were all kinds of pressures at play – arguments, business, money, married life – the tension at home was pretty obvious. My father was an only child and I think his parents doted on him and did not give him the important checks, balances and values needed while he was growing up. I suppose that, in the end, he just gave up and moved in with a new family. This taught me one simple thing: running away is a bad idea, no matter how hard life might be. If I ever became a parent myself, I was determined not to make the same mistakes. But at the time, I was largely able to ignore domestic problems by concentrating instead on my schooling and sport. I was not always a well behaved schoolboy and was once thrown out of a chemistry lesson by my teacher for seventy-eight minutes of an eighty minute double period for bad behaviour. He never did like me and the feeling was mutual. As far as I know, it is still a record. Another impressive teacher, Mr Ed Whall, also had very sharp eyes; he was frustrated by my actions and told me to give him a hundred lines in the morning, writing the following:

"It is most disconcerting to a well-regulated mind to see a young boy who ought to know better disporting himself wrongly at improper moments."

It took me a long time to write those lines. Aged thirteen or so, Mr Whall's words clearly had the desired effect. I didn't do it again.

During holidays, my wonderful Grandmother Caroline was always ready to take me in at her bungalow on the edge of Dartmoor, near Yelverton, after they left Honey Tor. I met up with the son whose family ran the local village shop. He and I would take regular trips on the bus from Clearbrook to Plymouth, where we would spend hours playing at the Snooker Club on Mutley Plain. He was much better than me and I rarely won a game. They were happy days and I looked up to my Grandmother and forward to my holidays a lot.

As I began my A-Level education, my thoughts turned to my future career. As both my godparents had sons in their families, taking on one of their farms was not really an option and, besides, I knew that it was not the lifestyle I wanted. I had neither the commitment nor knowledge to make a success of it. I tried an interview with the local bank manager who, quite rightly, said I needed something more challenging than an office life and I was told by the Devon and Somerset Police Force that I needed to grow a little to meet the height criteria. I didn't enjoy wearing the handcuffs either, so these visits both left me uncertain.

Time passed quickly with sufficient exam success and a new passion discovered through the Combined Cadet Force; it was either that or join the Band – easy decision! Fellow pupil David Suchet (later very well known in the part of the famous TV detective Poirot), had tried to teach me the drums. David was my schoolboy hero and very talented as an actor, musician and rugby player. I wanted to be as good as him and enjoyed watching his successes in later life. I would still like to meet him one day. Unfortunately, I have no sense of rhythm (although I'm told my enthusiastic banging of the steering wheel to accompany Dire Straits on the car radio never failed to entertain the children on long journeys).

Joining the Wellington School Cadet Force aged sixteen

was a welcome escape from the distractions at home. I enjoyed preparing and cleaning my kit for the day's activities, which included inspections, rudimentary drill parades and trips to the river to practice crawling across the crocodile-infested water on a self-built rope bridge, losing balance and recovering to complete the crossing (or getting wet for the unsuccessful). Easter and summer holidays saw us travelling to the Lake and Peak Districts and to Culttybraggan Camp in Perthshire, a place that had been used as a Prisoner of War camp during WW2. Mountain trekking and camping taught us how to live off what we could carry and to get to our destination despite the uncomfortable wind and rain. It was a satisfying, if occasionally testing, experience and we learned the value of good teamwork.

Our main trip in the summer of 1968 was a visit to the Army in West Germany, where we were hosted by the local Royal Signals Regiment and given a taste of military life by the soldiers. As part of our training programme, we went to see Bergen-Belsen Concentration Camp. Here was the place where hundreds of thousands of captives were held, starved, tortured and murdered during WW2. Many died through disease, typically Typhus; Anne Frank, author of her famous diary, died there. Bergen-Belsen was a huge camp where the entrance contained a small reception building, with gruesome photographs of the camp liberation in 1945. Outside, the pathway around the flat ground contained row upon row of burial mounds with small memorial stones saying: 10,000 Tot (dead), 3,000 Tot, and so on. There was an eerie silence, with no birdsong and a cold, haunting atmosphere. I had not been taught about it and so had no real knowledge of the World Wars of the 20th Century, nor the actions of our German adversaries, so I was not really able to grasp the tragedy and enormity of what I was witnessing. Neither did I appreciate that, just a mile or so away was Bergen-Hohne, the base of an Army armoured Brigade and its units that had been there since the end of the WW2. I was to see much more of those barracks and headquarters later. Today, Bergen-Belsen is a powerful memorial that I believe should be visited at least once by every European. It serves as a permanent reminder of the Holocaust and is a sobering place to experience, particularly by those who deny that it happened at all.

Aged seventeen, I came across a recruiting brochure discarded in a school common room at Wellington. It was a glossy white document with gold lettering – SANDHURST. The pictures looked exciting and the entry criteria was just two A-Levels. I was taking three – easy! I knew instantly that this was what I wanted to do. A familiarisation visit to the Royal Military Academy reinforced my eagerness.

And so it was. I achieved the three A-Level passes and left Wellington as House Captain. School days fostered similar bonds to those I later experienced in Service and I was sorry to say goodbye to good friends, particularly Gil Bray, a fellow House Captain and excellent rugby player. Our paths would cross again.

My early years at home and at school taught me how to live among a broken family who were struggling with a failed marriage and the tensions that came from that. I never spoke to anyone about my worries for the future and my teachers seldom raised the subject. I did become quiet and reserved but, fortunately, it was my experience in the Cadet Force and on the sports field that allowed me to forget my home life and grow in confidence.

In 1969, I applied to the Regular Commissions Board (RCB) at Westbury in Wiltshire to become an officer at The Royal Military Academy on a two-year training course. Accommodated in small single room blocks behind the very large and comfortable country house, a group of about eight candidates gathered for three testing days of physical and leadership potential. As one of the lightest and fittest in our group, I had little difficulty in getting around the assault course, could manage the walls and bridges easily and was quite happy to volunteer to go first. I was able to demonstrate a good grasp of current affairs and led an (unsuccessful) attempt to cross a wide gap using a few planks, some ropes and a bucket. The assessor gave me a good mark for briefing the group but said my estimate of time to complete the task was too ambitious. I went home after a final interview and awaited the result.

In the autumn of '69, I was offered a Regular Commission and a career for life, if I wanted it. It had lots of other benefits too but I didn't think too much about the pension at that time. I filled in the acceptance offer and prepared to go off to Sandhurst to join the Officer Cadet Intake in 1970.

To fill the time in between, I attended an eight-week outward bound course on Dartmoor, which was excellent for fitness preparation (daily runs down to the river and a cold dip at 06:00!), survival, canoeing skills, basic leadership and walks across Exmoor and Dartmoor leading a team of three as the final exercise. A summer sales job for a family of market stallholders (who would later go on to establish a famous high street clothing chain) taught me the importance of punctuality and helped me grow accustomed to early (very early) starts, though I knew I was never suited to be a businessman like my father.

With no previous military connection except an undercoat of CCF experience, I was excited by this next stage but had no idea of what was to follow. I arrived on Old College Square (the main parade ground at the Royal Military Academy, Sandhurst) in April 1970 on the appointed day the following spring, with a suitcase and an ironing board. I was to join a batch of eighteen to twenty-two year old Officer Cadets where some 80% of us were non-graduates, straight from school or college. As I retired in 2008, and was then responsible for the Academy, the proportion was almost entirely reversed with recruiters putting ever more emphasis on getting cadets with a degree education and reducing the time for officer training. I never felt that that was a sensible change; cadets needed the time to grow and mature into their future command role – time that is not always best made up through tertiary education and a curtailed training programme.

My reception at Sandhurst was a whirlwind. I disappeared for fourteen weeks.

LEAPS AND BOUNDS

A beautiful summer's day in 1971. We had bussed off to Weston-on-the-Green, a vast grassed area called the Landing Zone (LZ). Waiting there to greet us was our instructor and, 800 feet above, a large balloon with a basket hanging below it. The balloon was lowered and eight of us kitted up and climbed aboard. Secure in the balloon, we began the ascent. It was quiet up there, just the sound of the breeze in the canopy and a beautiful Oxfordshire countryside in view. The winch stopped.

Our instructor said, "Right gentlemen, who's first?"

I've always preferred to get a challenge over and done with, rather than watch others take the first leap (following a caving expedition during the outward bound course at age sixteen, I'd leapt off a bridge to get clean – at the invitation of our instructor – despite not being able to swim). By this point in my training, Sandhurst had also instilled in me the value and meaning of its motto, 'Serve to Lead'. So I volunteered for the balloon jump.

I stood up, secured my harness and walked to the basket door. An eerie silence.

The instructor said, "OK Sir?"

"Ready Flight Sergeant," I replied.

The rail was removed.

"RED ON!"

I gripped the safety bar and looked down to see the LZ and a crowd of people, 800 feet below.

"S**t!"

"GREEN ON, GO!"

I followed the drill that had been drummed into me, the descent was a blur for 120 feet as I plummeted like a stone. Mercifully, my parachute opened and I landed safely, walking off the LZ on a real high.

"Well done, sir," said my assessor. "Now, have a smoke and kit up, you'll be going up again in about an hour for the second jump."

Second? Really?

There were many high points during my time at Sandhurst – not all of them that literal, of course.

Innocent and wide-eyed, the first fourteen weeks of training had been a blur of activity based on performance standards, pass or fail, with most of it done on the run: very short haircuts, kit issues, inspections, fitness, drill and constant cleaning. (Jane struggles to believe the latter, having never seen me push a hoover around. But my clothes were always found in a neatly folded pile after a dinner night at the Mess).

Set in wonderful grounds at Camberley, Surrey, Sandhurst was formed in the 18th and 19th Centuries in response to various conflicts and world wars. At that time, it consisted of three colleges, with a large training area behind them: a huge parade ground was overlooked by Old College, redolent of Ancient Rome with its imposing façade of the pillars of Mars and Minerva and the famous steps, up which successful Officer Cadets would march to receive their commissions; New College, which was to be my home for the first year; and Victory College, where I finished the course. Concealed among the other buildings were the Gymnasium, swimming pool (I still hadn't learned to swim, so I needed a lot of training to pass that test), Memorial Chapel, shop and medical centre. Our doctor was Mick Molloy, a well-known Irish rugby international, who had hands like frying pans. Fortunately, a prostate exam wasn't part of the compulsory medical. In any event, we didn't go there much. It was not the 'done' thing to report sick.

My home for the first year in New College was to be a single room on the third floor at the top of the building. Fairly rudimentary facilities gave us room to hang our uniforms and other kit, secure our rifles (leaving them unlocked was a serious error and would lead to the award of show parades; parading before our head in full dress at 03:00 for a week was a fairly typical award). We soon learned to avoid them as any mistake found by the inspector, or being late, could lead to more days on parade. Our rooms were reached by three flights of stairs and we were given a very short time to Fall Out correctly, get upstairs and appear downstairs again, ready for the next part of the training programme ("On parade in three minutes – MOVE!"). Sprinting up the steep staircase with the other cadets was a bit of a struggle and sharp elbows were needed in the early days but the fitter we got, the easier it became. By the end of the day, our rooms were a complete shambles with kit all over the place. Getting it right was a real challenge but, slowly, we got to grips with the knack of keeping our room tidy and presenting our kit cleaned and ready for inspection for the next day. Being commended late one night for good, clean and pressed kit was very satisfying.

I had joined Ypres Company as part of Intake 48 with thirteen other cadets. We were forbidden from talking to each other until certain tests had been passed, which we were supposed to prepare for in our 'spare' time. Tests included the

Academy's layout and history and learning the names of the Academy staff: the Commandant, Major General Philip Tower, who won the Distinguished Service Order (DSO) for swimming the River Rhine during the Allied advance into Nazi Germany; the Company Commander; the Cadet Senior Under Officer of the Company; and our intake leader. By far the most imposing were the Academy Sergeant Majors, Mr Philips and Mr Huggins, the last of whom I met some thirty-six years later as a Chelsea Pensioner. Impressive gentlemen both – definitely not ones to upset.

But easily the scariest to us eighteen year old lads was Company Sergeant Major Frank Wells of the Welsh Guards. At well over 6ft tall, to me – standing at 5ft 7 – he was a very big man indeed, not to mention being the Army Heavyweight Boxing Champion, with the build (and nose) to show for it. Being stared at face-to-face (a distance guaranteed to frighten) by Sgt Major Wells, wielding a rifle with bayonet fixed and in the danger zone of my chin, accompanied by an ear-splitting, "You idle cadet, Mr Viggers, I'll run you through!" was an unforgettable experience. At first, I did my best to avoid him but he saw everything and, eventually, we became friends. He sold me his Mini car but he was so heavy that the suspension had a definite lean to the right.

While infantry skills, weapon handling and shooting formed a large part of our programme, drill, more drill and constant kit cleaning were the foundation of our training, teaching us the advantages of timekeeping (NEVER be late on parade), practice, concentration, instant obedience and teamwork – the fundamentals of platoon command. Initially, we were hopeless. But under the eagle eyes of our teacher, Colour Sergeant Terry Ewers of the Grenadier Guards, later to gain a Commission himself, we showed improvement on New College parade square. Gradually, after many hours of warm-ups known as 'rifting' – marching as a squad of thirteen around the parade square at pace, up and down with repeated about-turns, saluting, mark time, halts and off again – it started to come together. We even began to enjoy it. The team was working.

The highlight of our first term was the drill competition, when all the companies were inspected and taken through a well-practised routine of rifle and foot drill, rather like the annual Trooping the Colour Ceremony in London, all under the watchful gaze of our drill instructors. By then, our competitive, must-win spirit was fierce. We spent hours practising and were desperate to win. The rumour was that Ypres Company were good – very good. The day arrived and we marched over to Old College Square, performed our best and returned to the company block to await the result in the TV room. With fourteen teams to judge, it took time. As it was a fine spring day, the windows were open and we soon heard the unmistakable footfall of Sergeant Major Wells approaching. Sticking his head round the door, in his unmistakable Welsh growl, he simply said, "Well done gentlemen, you b******s have won!"

Fourteen companies in the competition and we were the best of all. We were ecstatic. We did it for our instructors, who took us to the Hero of Inkerman Pub in Bagshot (long since closed down) to celebrate over curry and beer. When we got home very early in the morning, Frank was in bits; he couldn't speak and we weren't much better. But we had realised that, finally, we were a good team and we knew the joy of winning. I never lost that sense. From then on, whenever we needed transport to go out on exercise, Ypres Company got first pick of the four-tonne lorries to get us there.

Soon, the first fourteen weeks of training at the Academy ended and we had passed. All those Cadets who started Term 1 were still there but, had I been told that I hadn't done well enough and would be 'back-termed' for a second try, I am convinced that I would have left the course. I was badly in need of a break and to get the chance to go home. Repeating the experience just wasn't worth it. I am sure it was the team spirit that had been created by our instructors in drill, weapon handling and physical training that had carried us to the end and we all enjoyed the sense of achievement. I was fitter, more confident and felt that I 'belonged' to a good gang of young men. We still had lots to learn but the seeds of successful leadership had been sown.

As we emerged successfully from our basic training, the pace of the first term slackened significantly. The academy returned from leave and we entered the academic year. We undertook studies of language, history of war, technology and shooting. Sport and fitness featured significantly in the programme and I played rugby, mainly with Johnny Kaye and Steve Thomas, almost every day. Marvellous! Steve was a talented Welshman. With a Welsh grandmother, we had a lot in common and got on very well. We were expected to be reliable, to turn up as and when required, on time and ready to do whatever was asked of us, again all under the exacting scrutiny of our instructors, which in itself was good training. Competitions continued and we narrowly lost the Assault Course Race to the hot favourites.

After our success in the drill competition, we badly wanted to win the assault course and spoke to our physical training instructor. He was an Olympian triathlon competitor, a great example and super fit. Reassuring him that we were deadly serious and would turn up for his daily training sessions, he agreed to take us on, get us fit, and teach us the techniques of obstacle crossing, rope climbing and teamwork. We turned up as ordered, gave it our best and soon, the rumour was that Ypres Company were favourite to win.

As the day arrived, we got the bad news. We learned that our cadet from overseas had returned to the Academy in the early hours after a night on the town in London. We didn't know what he had been up to and he wouldn't say (but we could guess that it wasn't designed to get him alert and ready), and it was clear that he was in no real shape for the race. But because he knew the drills he had to carry out to get us around, we decided to risk it and hope that he would finish the course, followed by the squad run over a mile to the rifle range, and the ten round shoot at 300M range, with hits to count. The whistle went and he started well enough. We completed the assault course without injury in a good, fast time. We set off for the run and, approaching the top of the hill, he fell and said he could not go on. Picking him up, we redistributed his kit. I took his rifle and we set off again, hauling him with us. We reached the range breathless, put ten rounds into our magazines and took up firing positions. We fired and awaited the results. They were acceptable but not as good as previous shoots had been. We had been let down by our badly-behaved overseas cadet and we came second. Wisely, someone took the cadet away from us and it was a while before we saw him again. Probably a good thing, and I learned a good lesson that day about commitment to the task.

As the course progressed, regular parades were held at the Memorial Chapel. Later in life, this place came to be of special importance to me but, even back then, I never ceased to be impressed by its grandeur and the memory of so many comrades and fellow officers who had given their lives in great wars and other conflicts and whose names were listed on the columns around us.

Soon, the time came when we were asked to select the Regiment we would like to join. With no previous military experience, I didn't really know what I wanted. I wrestled with this choice. I knew what I didn't want – the Infantry (too much digging) – and where it didn't feel right; the Cavalry. And I knew who my friends were (Dave Wallace, Steve Thomas, to name just two) and they were all asking to join the Royal Artillery – The

Gunners. So I applied, attended the interview (in rugby kit) and was accepted. Relief. I now knew where I was going. Thomas and Wallace were accepted too.

Life at the Academy had its more amusing moments as we enjoyed the opportunity to get away. Mostly we had fun but, generally, our high spirits did not lead to anything serious. Thomas and I did on one occasion stay out until too late and, creeping back with a take away meal, Thomas said that he knew of a way to get in to New College without breaking the locks. We crept quietly around to the rear of the building, where we slid back the grill to the cellar entrance below. We began to climb down in the dark...

"Stand fast gentlemen," said the guard, a military policeman with a big dog emitting a low, chilling growl.

"Does your dog like Chinese?" asked Thomas, soberly and innocently.

"No, sir," he replied, "Only cadets. Come with me."

Keeping a diplomatic separation between us and the dog, he escorted us back to the front door of the building, gave us a stern telling off and let us in. We enjoyed our Chinese and, as far as I can recall, we heard no more of it. Lucky. Both of us could have been on show parades for weeks after that.

As the summer term of '71 and leave approached, we were encouraged to do something adventurous. That's how I'd ended up jumping out of the balloon. Another cadet in our company, John Martin, persuaded me to attend the Parachute Course based at Abingdon. We reported and embarked on a course of repetitive training, jumping, rolling, landing – all according to the drills hammered into us by our RAF instructor. Obedience and trust became second nature; we completed two practice jumps from the balloon and were assessed as ready to complete our first descent from a Hercules.

The very next weekend, I was to make a leap of an entirely different kind.

With the luxury of a couple of days off, John and I decided to go to his house, near St Albans. On the Saturday evening, we drove into town for a beer. As we were looking for a parking space, I saw a girl walking with her friend. She looked at me. The effect was electric. Without doubt, she was the most beautiful girl I had ever seen. I stared at her, she raised her eyebrow at me and we drove on. *Who was that?* I thought.

We parked and were walking towards the pub, when there she was again. We walked along. Eye-to-eye, "Do you have a light?" I asked (not my most gallant moment). Her reply, quick as a flash, "Yes. Do you have a cigarette?" The perfect 'match'. So we went for a drink, she gave me her number and I went home.

Jane was unforgettable and I was determined to see her again.

FIRST TOUR

As the final term at Sandhurst arrived in 1972, the crisis in Northern Ireland reached a head. Thousands were being deployed to the Province, and particularly 'Bandit Country', where the IRA operated often violently against what they saw as an occupying force.

At Sandhurst, we cadets knew that we would soon be there ourselves, usually in Londonderry (known by most of us as Derry), Belfast or on the known hot spots along the border, in command of our platoons. It gave training a real edge. The IRA was killing our soldiers.

Added impetus was given to our final infantry exercise in the UK and Cyprus, refining our military skills and, most importantly, preparing for the Sovereign's Parade in March 1972, when we would be commissioned into our Regiments as Second Lieutenants.

Our first major ten-day exercise was to take place at Sennybridge Camp in Wales. Purchased by the War Office in 1939, Sennybridge was the third-largest training camp in the UK and was renowned for its unpredictable weather conditions. Rain was guaranteed. Our instructors told us that, on our arrival, we would deploy straight on to the area and operate from patrol bases. All the basic skills would be tested, including preparing defensive positions, patrolling and ambushes, attacking the enemy. We would have a variety of command appointments and should be prepared to live in the cold and wet. Hypothermia was a real risk and, badly managed, could result in serious injury or worse.

I had seen the effects of hypothermia during my Outward Bound Course, two years before, so I knew its dangers and what I needed to do to avoid the risk. Returning for a weekend at Jane's home, I asked if I could borrow a few pairs of tights. Having no real experience of military life, other than her brothers who had completed National Service, she was obviously surprised at this question and probably wondered why on earth I wanted them and who she was dating anyway. I explained where I was going and she provided me with a couple of pairs.

The doom-mongers were right. It rained day after day for our time in Sennybridge and, on the rare occasions it stopped, the midges at our patrol bases in the damp, dark forests had a voracious appetite. They would not leave us alone and it was a real test to ignore their buzzing and biting as we tried to focus on what we were doing. Tempers were in short supply and a sense of humour was a definite bonus. Thankfully, the tights worked and kept me warm at night but, after a day's soaking, they would not dry out and I would carry on with wet boots until I could change. Eventually, everything we carried with us was wet and heavy but we just became used to living in those conditions. From then on, whenever we faced difficult or uncomfortable situations, I would just think, "It's not as bad as Sennybridge", and that put my job in context. As things turned out, it would not be the only time I needed tights in my career, either.

The exercise in Cyprus was testing and had a memorable moment. Our training instructors were teaching us the skills and techniques of a night fighting patrol and the execution of an ambush. Complicated and testing stuff, if we were to get it right. We were taken through the packing and carrying of our kit, so that our movement across country was silent. Jumping up and down revealed the mistakes. We did a dress rehearsal of the placing and layout in silence, and the triggering of the ambush.

It was hard, thirsty work in the heat of the Cypriot sun and, as we were given a rest, our instructor turned to one of our overseas cadets. He came from Uganda. "Will you tell us?" he asked. "How you do a night ambush in your country?"

"No, I cannot," he replied in his unmistakable accent. "We do not fight at night. Because of the lions." The instructor moved on, unblinking, to the next stage. Ever since, a posting to Africa somehow lost its appeal for me.

We were in full rehearsal for weeks leading up to the Sovereign's Parade. At the dress rehearsal, we were slow marching up the steps of Old College, in three ranks and with the Academy Band playing, when all of a sudden the unmistakable bass tones of Frank Wells's successor, and another Welsh Guard, Company Sergeant Major Danny Hearn, assaulted our ears from directly behind. To the tune of 'God Bless the Prince of Wales', he sang, "You three get your hair cut, do you understand?" Unexpected, but hilarious. He told us to be quiet.

Duly shorn, the day of the Commission Parade arrived. As we began rehearsals, we learned that our senior cadet was unable to lead our intake during the Commissioning parade and I was tasked to replace him. I had taken part in many of these events and was very familiar with the routine and orders I would have to give, so I was not worried about it. It was a great pity that the real parade leader had to miss out on the occasion and many of us were disappointed that he couldn't be there. He was a good leader and we had his confidence but it did show that a fall back Plan B was always needed should the unexpected arise. That learning would come to my aid later on.

The Queen Mother was the Royal Guest. Jane, her father and my mother came to watch. It was a big day and a big deal. We'd cracked it. We had completed two years of demanding training among cadets and instructors whom I would not forget, and this all came together in a Parade that was to sum up our achievements. We marched up the steps of Old College, followed by the Adjutant on his white charger.

Looking back to the 1970s, Sandhurst was for me an outstanding training system. An intake of mainly non-graduates with minimal military experience were taken on a course of character building and leadership development. Standards were high and not reaching them was not acceptable. Those who fell short were removed. Thankfully, of the thirteen of us who started, all but one completed the course. I made some friends for life and learned lessons I would not forget about how to lead and inspire soldiers. Respect, obedience and loyalty were a given and drummed into us from start to end. Success came from winning and could only be achieved through dedication. These were the things that stuck with me throughout my life and I learned quickly how to follow those of my superiors who had these qualities. Those who did not were not worth their weight.

After summer leave, I completed Young Officer training at The Royal School of Artillery, Larkhill. The course taught me a great deal about the skills and techniques of Gunnery and what I was to expect when I reported to my Regiment. There was a good bunch of students and we enjoyed a fun time, not all of it on our best behaviour. After one particularly alcoholic evening we decided to drive to Stonehenge to upset the annual Druid's assembly at the summer solstice. We managed to break into the car park without attracting attention, started some vehicles and set off for the A303 in the dark. Suddenly, we were stopped by the military police. The soldier looked at the driver and said, "Have you had any experience of driving this vehicle, sir?" The driver replied, "About five minutes, Corporal." We were escorted back to the garages and told to parade in front of the Commandant in the morning.

We paraded and were told in no uncertain times how badly behaved we had been. Fortunately, no one was injured and, as punishment that we were to treat as a lesson learned, we were told to sell £25 worth of raffle tickets by Monday, or produce the cash if we couldn't. That gave us forty-eight hours over the weekend – difficult. I went off to see Jane and paid up in cash. Much easier that way.

Weekends on leave were spent meeting Jane's family (a complicated business! With ten older brothers, I knew I needed to behave myself). I also took her off to meet my folks on the family farm near Launceston – we were getting quite serious then. Her hay bale tossing skills passed muster and my godmother and her family approved. Jane accepted my proposal and our future together was set in train.

I was posted to 38 (Seringapatam) Battery in 40 Regiment Royal Artillery, based in Gutersloh, West Germany. The homes of the British and American forces mirrored largely the positions occupied in Germany by the Allies at the end of WW2, with the British in the north-west and the Americans in the south. Barracks were based in towns on the sites built under Hitler's regime and occupied by Nazi air and land forces – large accommodation blocks capable of housing thousands of troops and able to last for hundreds of years, with messes, stores and offices to cater for the officers and non-commissioned ranks.

Our own Regimental headquarters was said to be haunted by a German officer who patrolled the silent corridors in a long, dark-grey trench-coat. Duty clerks reported hearing his footsteps and the 'Grey Man' became part of the legend of Gutersloh's Mansergh Barracks. Walking the camp area at night on security patrol was certainly an eerie experience. I didn't see the Grey Man but others swore to having sensed his presence and seen shadows in the dark.

We spent many weeks in our deterrent role, training and practising firing across the training areas in Germany as part of the Cold War. The Status of Forces Agreement, signed after WW2, allowed us to train and move through the selected villages, fields and countryside of North West Germany; large areas were agreed for our exercises when live firing was not required. These 'dry' exercises usually lasted two or three weeks and were generally enjoyable. They allowed me to develop the skills I had picked up during the Young Officers' course as our Regiment conducted its firing drills, moved to new gun positions and conducted river crossings over bridges built by the Royal Engineers, almost always at night.

For training involving live firing, we had the use of two ranges, both of which had evidence of the German Army (the Wehrmacht) during WW2. Munsterlager had a small impact area on which we could fire, while Bergen-Hohne (where I'd visited as a Cadet) was much larger with a bigger selection of gun positions and a much bigger target or impact area. This was a favourite place for Hitler to review his troops, with large bunkers and a ring road surrounding the area. The Germans were quick to spot an opportunity and supporting the gun crews was a camper van providing a selection of German sausages (Bratwurst), chips, coffee and other snacks. Often, as we were preparing to move from one place to another, the van owner would shout "WOHER?" – where? – "Gun position", or "GP 18", we would shout to him as we were packing up and, to our surprise, he would usually be there as we arrived, tucked into the woods and ready to serve the soldiers. The bratty wagon became a well-used and popular facility. The owner did very well on the proceeds too.

It was to emerge later that Peter Bonnet, my Battery

Commander, protected me from much of the nonsense that was going on in the Regiment above me: the Commanding Officer was an aloof individual, with little time for his subordinates (he said nothing to me for months after I arrived). I saw how demoralised his men had become and realised how they felt bullied, humiliated and undervalued by him. He was not at all respected, resulting in much discontent among the younger officers: a number left the army or talked about asking for a transfer.

Peter protected me from that. He taught me how to plan, lead and inspire young soldiers – lessons I would not forget. I was responsible for about forty young Gunners in the Regiment, most of whom had a Scottish background. They were tough men who lived and played hard. Peter insisted that I got to know them by keeping a troop notebook with me, showing the facts about my men: their personal and family details, pay and next of kin, planned career courses and future promotion prospects. I interviewed all of them and it did help to get to know their story.

Peter called me in to his office one day and asked me to produce my notebook. Fortunately, it was with me and up to date. Then he told me that it was time to learn what happens at a Court Martial. A Gunner soldier in the Battery was being brought up on an Absence Without Leave charge and he wanted me to act as his Defending Officer. Giving me the outline, he sent me to the guardroom and told me to interview the soldier in the cells and write the Plea in Mitigation. I did my best and showed it to Peter, who made some amendments. The plea was much the better for it and I went with the soldier to the Court Martial Centre. I listened to the President hear the charge. He did not look happy and it did not look good for the soldier. Eventually, he called me up to read the Plea. I laid on the sympathy story as honestly and thickly as I could, explaining that it had been a big misunderstanding, that he was a good man really and that his family would be distraught if he were to be given a lengthy sentence. He had learned his lesson; needed a break so that he could get his career back on track. The President said nothing and the Board adjourned to deliberate its findings. At the end, the soldier was called in, the guilty verdict was proven, I was thanked for giving a persuasive plea and the President awarded a very lenient custodial sentence – much lighter than he might have delivered. By the time I got back to the barracks, I had become a hero: "If you're on a charge and in trouble, ask for Mr Viggers to be your Defending Officer – he gets results!"

As expected, a tour to Northern Ireland soon arrived and we embarked on some demanding training, including shooting, fitness, check points and patrolling skills. We deployed to Londonderry for four months. As we crossed Craigavon Bridge over the River Foyle on our way to our new base at Fort George, I asked my driver if he knew where to go. "Yes, sir," he replied before turning left. *That's odd*, I thought, *I'm sure he should have turned right*. It didn't feel or look good as we drove on in my covered Landrover and my fears were confirmed as a rock bounced off the side with a loud crack, not unlike a gunshot. Looking out of the windscreen, I saw the famous graffiti on the house wall:

YOU ARE NOW ENTERING FREE DERRY.

Rocks and abuse thrown and shouted by young kids continued to rain down on us as we made an emergency three point turn and left at speed back to the bridge. We were lucky that day; if there had been armed terrorists out there, the IRA would have had a success before the tour had hardly started. Wisely, the driver didn't say much as we drove back to the base. He didn't need to.

My task while I was there was to organise the manning

of the border Vehicle Check Point on the road to Buncrana, County Donegal in the Irish Republic. The Army had two men on the most wanted IRA list: Gerry Adams was a known Belfast-based terrorist and Martin McGuiness, an IRA commander who hailed from the Bogside estate in Londonderry, where rioting yobs would trouble our patrols regularly. It was reported that Adams was living in a well-off part of Belfast and travelled freely around the city, while McGuiness was once photographed talking to one of our young officers at a checkpoint. So we knew they were there and active but somehow they eluded capture and arrest. We will never know how much damage and pain they went on to cause during the Troubles.

I had a team of four to six men at the checkpoint there for twenty-four hours every day and we relieved them in shifts. My troop checked all the vehicles crossing the border for weapons and explosives and watched a house on the high ground over the border that we believed had been used to shoot at our protected bunker. Those travelling through the checkpoint and being searched were usually surly and occasionally aggressive. We were clearly not welcome there and my brother officers were getting a hard time in the other areas, like the Bogside and Shantallow Estates, where riots were a common feature. I was nervous about becoming too predictable as we drove my soldiers to begin their shift, so we did our best to change our routine by altering the times of changeover, patrolling to the site or setting up observation posts to watch over likely ambush spots along the route. Keeping my lads focused was not difficult and they worked hard at maintaining their skills while off duty.

Just across the road from our check point was a large house occupied by a delightful couple. He had been a very successful and well-known businessman and was enjoying his retirement. As Protestants living in a predominantly Catholic community, we saw a potential threat to their safety. They were defenceless senior citizens and I made sure that my soldiers kept an eye on them, visited them regularly, calling on them for coffee and chatting to re-assure them. A few weeks into our tour, my Troop Sergeant Major Kev Trow and I were invited to their house for dinner. We thought about this and believed that, provided it was properly arranged, it was a low-risk invite and we accepted. Peter was happy for me to go and we made sensible contingencies to cover the time I was away. The date arrived, a patrol mounted a permanent guard around the house and we drove to their home. We both carried a loaded 9mm pistol and I concealed mine in my waistband under my jacket. We were shown into and around their house and our hosts were very generous. I sat down, hoping that the pistol would not fall out and, as we were about to then move through to the dining room, his wife, with her arm on mine and a concerned look on her face, said quietly in a soft Irish whisper:

"Why don't you leave your gun on the sideboard, dear? You'll be much more comfortable sitting down then."

Feeling found out and just a little embarrassed, I did as she asked. Kev Trow, as my bodyguard, declined. We thoroughly enjoyed our time with them and I returned with my pistol safe and no harm done. But once was enough and, knowing how fast the rumour gets around Derry, we decided not to push our luck too much. Fortunately, the invite wasn't repeated.

On one bright day, when our mood was good, I picked my time and approached Peter. He and his wife Sylvia were delightful people and made a huge difference to my approach and outlook. Here was a man I could respect as a leader. In accordance with the convention: "Peter", I asked, "if it is all right with you, Jane and I would like to get married during my leave." His reaction was instant – and also very much 'of the time' in his assessment of Jane's 'suitability' as an Army wife. "Marvellous. Jane will be a great addition to our Wives' Club! Of course, you can." What I did not know was that, when Peter informed the Commanding Officer of my request, he refused; no married quarter would be available to us until I qualified for one by marriage and perhaps the CO felt, despite never having met her, that at age 16 and 21 respectively, Jane and I were too young. Peter did not tell me this until years later and, when I knew that he'd protected us from that, I had even more respect for him. Our wedding plans went ahead.

At the half way point, we were interrupted as we moved to Belfast to keep the Protestant and Catholic communities apart. My Battery was allocated a largely Protestant area that had a heavy Ulster Defence Association presence – really hard men who hated the Catholics and were well-organised – with the small village of Ligoniel on the outskirts. I had a troop base there to protect the isolated Catholic community. I spent my time patrolling these areas to provide reassurance and deter violence. It was difficult to reason with these people as the Catholics hated us and the Protestants saw us as friendly, sent by the UK to keep the Province stable. The other Batteries had an equally difficult time dealing with the different communities. We faced a determined IRA and they were testing times but mercifully there were no real disasters.

The end of the Ireland tour came quickly enough and we returned to the UK for some summer leave. Jane had been doing most (all) of the work to prepare for our wedding, planned for 14th July – Bastille Day – in Welshpool. I had two tasks and they were important: get a suit and sort out a Best Man. Although my old school friend Gil Bray and I had exchanged the odd letter, we hadn't really stayed in touch in that time, but I was confident that he was a good man whom I could trust, who would look after us if the need ever arose. And that has certainly proved to be the case later in life. Fortunately, he agreed to the mission immediately. Good decision! I would repay the favour in 1974 when Gil married Caroline (known to us all as 'Twink') and I was his best man – they remain our closest friends to this day. Twink is a Cornish girl from Launceston so we had a lot in common from the start.

The big day arrived. We were ready and the really good news was that Jane's father, who had not been at all well, had recovered and was fit enough to escort Jane down the aisle and hand her to me. I've never been that confident about living up to the important occasion and that was a big day, no doubt. Jane looked stunning and the day flew by. We spent our honeymoon in Hereford and seeing family friends until it came time for us to get back to the Regiment after leave.

One of the advantages of marrying into the Army at that time was that Jane was able to build a support network of other wives in the same situation, few of whom had careers of their own and so expected and wanted to immerse themselves in Army life and work together to handle the pressures of being a soldier's wife – sub-standard accommodation, separation, money worries, lone parenting to name a few. Jane is very socially accomplished and a resilient, competent person, so despite her initial nervousness about entering 'the life', she dealt admirably with every challenge thrown at her. Our experiences as a young, married couple were a key factor in my commitment to improving the quality of life for soldiers and their families when I was commanding and, much later, as Adjutant General.

The two of us started out broke but happy. We had been allocated a tiny, one bedroom flat in Gutersloh. Our introduction to the Regiment was a whirl of parties, sport and formal occasions. When Jane was introduced to the Commanding Officer (the same one who'd refused our marriage request), his opening question to her was "Do you shoot?" It was the only time he ever spoke to her (Jane later said that she wished she'd responded, "Only COs."). Given that she grew up a town girl with no countryside experience at all, anyone who had done his research would know that this was a ridiculous question; I have no idea what he was trying to say, or prove. A quote I once heard seemed apt in this situation – you have my loyalty, you have to earn my respect. I couldn't respect a leader who treated all of us like inferior 'idiot boys'. Not for the first time, I thought about applying for a transfer from the Gunners to another Regiment but, fortunately, that CO's successor was a huge improvement because he took a real interest in those under his command. Another good lesson for me in leadership, and one that I would always try to remember and apply if I was to be a CO myself.

Our trip to BATUS (the British Army Training Unit Suffield) in Canada was a particularly good experience, as was our victory in the Regiment's Best Gun competition. I was to exercise in Canada twice more and, this time, we were supporting the Scots Guards. The training area in Canada was a huge prairie of dried up lakes and plains grasses thirty miles from Medicine Hat, Alberta. It is a vast place, once used as a weapons research establishment. Explosions were measured by the effects at ten, twelve and fifteen mile circles, identified by marked tracks and signed on the map. The drive to the start of the fifteen-day exercise could take hours. In summer, the weather is very hot indeed and, fanned by the breeze, the dry grasses present a real fire hazard. It is a demanding test of navigational, logistical, medical and administrative skills. In contrast, the winter can arrive without warning, snow falls are feet deep, drifting occurs and can lead to freezing conditions, where vehicles have to be marked and left until the spring thaw arrives. Survival becomes a real challenge for those unlucky enough to get caught out.

BATUS was a demanding exercise that required us to use all our skills and we enjoyed it but the experience was marred by one worrying incident. As I arrived back in Germany, Jane was not where I expected her to be. I was told to go and see the doctor; John Jones was in the Royal Air Force and attached to our Regiment to look after the soldiers and their families. He and his wife Liz became very good friends to us. While I was in Canada, Jane felt very unwell and, rather than send her home, John insisted that she should stay with them. That night, she collapsed. It was a miscarriage and it could have killed her. I was so lucky to have such a caring man looking after us. We have stayed in touch.

On exercise back in Germany, the Best Gun competition was to be a high point of the first tour for me. In all, eighteen guns entered and were put through the full range of technical Gunnery, tactical and military skills with a good spread of physical fitness thrown in. My gun commanders, six of them, wanted to win and be as highly placed as possible. Come the day, not only did we win the 'Best Gun overall', we won the next five places too. A total of six out of six – remarkable! We'd trained hard for it. Winning mattered and morale was high at the after party.

The next two years of our lives passed with me away more on training courses than I was at home. Thankfully, Jane was able to deal with my absences wonderfully (or so it appeared to me; she never complained). As we started 1975, Jane told me that she was expecting a child, due in September. This was brilliant news. The only downside was that I had another tour in Northern Ireland approaching and a second posting soon after that. This could be a close run thing but, once again, Jane just got on with it and was cheerful and supportive throughout. I needed that. It was just what was expected at the time; soldiers went away, came back and went away again. Not all the wives coped as they were 'expected' to – I regret that I took Jane's support for granted too much and I'm not proud of that.

For our impending tour to Northern Ireland, Peter said that he wanted me to become his Intelligence Officer, gave me a team of two and sent me off to my Intelligence Officer's course in the UK to prepare for the deployment. Over a fairly intensive three weeks' training, we were taught the basic skills of intelligence gathering, assessments and report writing. For the final exercise, I was tasked to meet a source at an obvious place in the local city, listen to his information and submit my report on return. I walked around the area and spotted a prominent garage selling new and second hand cars. There on the forecourt was an immaculate pink Rolls Royce. *Perfect*, I thought, *there can't be too many of these for sale and it's an obvious place to meet.* Hiding the time and place of the meeting in the dead letter drop, I returned to the garage and prepared to meet my source. I used up the time by pretending to inspect the car while awaiting his arrival. The source (one of my instructors) appeared at the right time, we made eye contact and, as I was about to walk away and lead him to a secure place, the salesman appeared and tried to sell me the car. I told him I wasn't interested but he would not give up, inviting me to take a seat, look at the controls and check the boot. The source saw all this going on and my impatience in trying to get away from this very keen salesman. He was still laughing at me after I made my escape and, at the debrief, said that I had done everything right – except finding a good place. So, be ready for the unexpected. I remembered that.

Our second tour to Ireland was in Belfast. Our Battery was based in a place called the Gasworks in the city, alongside the Ormeau Road, containing large gas-filled containers rather like the Oval cricket ground. Porta-cabin accommodation and rudimentary facilities – cookhouse, ablutions, laundry – dotted the ground nearby. We had a troop away from our area on detachment commanded by Lt Chris Nicholls, an impressive operator, living in the Mission Hall adjoining a Catholic enclave called The Markets. This had been a risky area and the IRA was known to be active. The streets were full of cramped housing lived in by struggling, poor people with large, complicated family structures. We were neither popular nor respected there.

The IRA had declared a ceasefire as we arrived and we spent our days on re-assurance, patrolling and searching for hidden weapons. We were helped in this by a highly impressive team from the Royal Ulster Constabulary and I got to work closely with them and know them well. There were a few moments of high drama. One day, an unknown bomber placed a flask bomb inside a Land Rover parked outside the Hall. The noise was deafening but, thankfully, the old place was still standing and no-one was hurt. Unstirred by this, we carried on. Peter Bonnet gave us strong direction and focus and, as his Intelligence Officer working with the police team, I thoroughly enjoyed my time there. We had a good tour, with one small fright...

There was a code known by us all– RATTRAP. This call over the radio meant one thing. *Orders: get to the nearest main road as fast as possible and stop the traffic. Number plate to follow – bad people were on the move.* We were on patrol very early one morning. It was pitch black and silent, apart from the occasional barking dog. "RATTRAP!" We ran, fast, to the road ahead. Suddenly, a loud crash and I'm flying through the air, landing winded in a heap. "Man down" over the radio and all went quiet. *A trap? A sniper?* The lads gathered round me, rifles covering the arcs. "You OK?" "Yes, fine." I got up and shone a light… I had run into an abandoned pram. A broken knuckle and wounded pride was the price I paid, and I took some stick for that.

One of my tasks on Saturdays was to chair the regular meeting of the joint military and police security teams. Peter attended with representatives of the Royal Ulster Constabulary and their Special Branch and we would review the activities of the week, co-ordinate our future events and assess and act on any intelligence that the SB had picked up. Sensing that the Battery's soldiers were becoming a bit stale after a number of weeks on patrol, I asked my SB rep to give us a tip about a weapon hide. Finding a weapon would give the other patrols a real lift and keep them keen. The SB man promised to see what he could do. He came back to the meeting the following week, gave me an address and described where a rifle and ten rounds of ammunition were well-concealed. I passed the details to one of my patrols and they planned the task. The search was conducted at night and the patrol came back with the rusty rifle and nine rounds.

I waited for the next Saturday and, at the right moment, thanked the SB for the tip and said that it was almost spot on because my patrol came back with the rifle and only nine rounds. He smiled, reached into his jacket pocket and handed me the tenth round saying, "My contact tells me that your boys left one behind. Bad luck." He bested me that day and I vowed not to tease him again. The SB were better than that and it was something of an own goal.

Ahead of Easter, 1975, we began to plan for the security of the Loyalist Orange Marches. Accompanied by bands of pipes and drums, young baton throwers and triumphalist music, the Orange Order would parade through the streets of Belfast wearing sashes to remember William of Orange and assert their right to parade. This was a potentially dangerous event as the marchers would arrive at the Catholic community and do all they could to intimidate the observers. Put the two together and major disturbance, riots and serious injury were a real possibility. The Protestant marchers themselves were also at risk because Catholics could open fire as the column and bands went past. To keep the two apart, we deployed huge screens of corrugated metal, mounted on four-tonne lorries, to mask off the roads and streets along the marching route and placed observers at the vulnerable points to deter any snipers. The RUC were there in strength on the day and walked alongside the column to keep it moving. Our plan worked and the march went well but I saw serried ranks of marchers hurling abuse and throwing items like billiard balls, darts and other risks to life and limb over the screens. The hatred was palpable, and I thought that the Troubles had a long way to go before a peaceful settlement could be reached.

In the summer of 1975, one of our guard section was manning an observation post high up at the top of one of the gasworks towers. The guard's task was to observe the pub on the street below the tower, just around the corner from the Ormeau Bridge. The pub was in a Catholic stronghold and at risk from Protestants intent on doing harm to anyone inside. It was a quiet afternoon with little activity, until a car appeared, paused as two suspicious-looking men got in, and drove off again. The car reappeared and the same men dismounted, walked into an alleyway and returned to stand by the door of the pub. Holding what looked like a canister, the men lit a match but it went out. It lit on the second attempt and one man opened the door and rolled the canister into the pub. It failed to go off and the men ran back to the car. Observing all this, the watch commander ordered the newly-joined young gunner to fire on the escaping terrorists. Two shots rang out and both men were hit. They got back in the car and drove off at speed, shooting at and narrowly avoiding another patrol. The car was found soon afterwards with the two men, both Protestants, inside; one dead and the other badly wounded. Bravely, a pub customer had picked up the canister and thrown it into the railway cutting and it was later disabled by the Army's Ammunition Technical Officer. The Battery's Quick Reaction Force deployed in a hurry to follow up any after-effects but the incident soon quietened down and the Battery emerged with great credit, particularly because of the cool, calm actions of the young gunner on duty. We demonstrated our determination and impartiality and

Peter used the example on a number of occasions to good effect.

As our tour came to an end, Peter Bonnet left the Battery and I was soon to follow to be posted to the Junior Leaders Regiment based in Bramcote, near Nuneaton. This posting, while not unwelcome, was to provide a surprise for me two years later. During our Young Officer's Course being conducted after commissioning, we were told that we would have some flexibility when deciding where to go for our second posting. We were even encouraged to go for a 'funny' – to try parachuting, another artillery discipline overseas or riding with The King's Troop Royal Horse Artillery. My career managers asked me what I would like to do and I said I would like to complete the Commando course and be posted to 29 Commando Regiment based in Plymouth. This would allow me to return with Jane to the South West, link up with my family and play rugby at Launceston in Cornwall when time allowed. My managers' response was that there were no vacancies left in Plymouth for second tour officers and so I could not go. I was later to learn from a Battery Commander in 29 that he was screaming out for a new officer and would have taken me immediately. I also discovered that I could, in fact, volunteer for Commando training and my request would have to be honoured. Hearing about that was frustrating and I felt that my managers had let me down. They had been less than honest in their advice. Perhaps they were worried about filling known vacancies in the Junior Leaders Regiment and told me an untruth. I will never know but it did teach me that I should not always accept things at face value.

After my three year tour with my first Regiment, I felt that I had had a good posting. I had learned the fundamentals of being a good artilleryman, knew what the men in the Battery had to do and how the larger Regiment worked. I began to grasp the needs and actions of deterrence during the Cold War in West

Germany and of Irish terrorism at home. Peter Bonnet taught me some valuable techniques about command and leadership, skills that I would not forget. Jane and I also made some good friends in 40 Regiment, many of whom we would see again.

So, off I went to Nuneaton, oblivious to how things might have been. But, as things turned out in the future, I really have no complaints (and might not have passed the Commando Course anyway).

Jane, with weeks to go before the baby was due, settled us in. She was admitted to hospital in September 1975, where, after quite a struggle, our son Brendan was born. No fridge was provided in the Army quarter; she put his bottles of milk out on the windowsill to keep them cold.

EARLY LESSONS IN LEADERSHIP:
BRAMCOTE AND J (SIDI REZEGH) BATTERY, ROYAL HORSE ARTILLERY

"What are your hobbies, Junior Gunner Corker?" I asked.

"Osses, sir."

"Say again?"

"Osses. I breed osses. For racing."

Corker, a ginger-haired, football-mad lad from the North East, was known from then on as Geordie Corker. He was a typical Junior Leader who appeared among a large group of fifteen to sixteen year old boys at Bramcote each September. Those who didn't leave after three months (about half decided it wasn't for them) stayed with us for the rest of the year and went on to join their first Artillery Regiments. I was made responsible for fifty of these young Gunners, the members of Ironside Troop. My time was spent planning, teaching and watching their training, interviewing them – usually working into the night – and looking out for the recruits who showed promise to act eventually as examples, mentors and positive role models. Paul Corker was one. Nigel (Taff) Kalies another.

The Juniors' training was demanding and not unlike the kinds of things we did at Sandhurst. A variety of training methods sustained their interests and the recruits were given time to learn. We developed their strength and fitness in readiness to go away for a week of adventure training in a cottage near the village of Betws y Coed in Snowdonia. Their activities resembled the Outward Bound Course I completed as a schoolboy, with runs, early morning swims in the very cold and fast flowing streams, canoeing, trekking and camping. Leading my team to the summit of Snowdon was a good achievement and gave the recruits a real sense of teamwork and mutual support. It was a good exercise and the instructors enjoyed the occasional visit to the local pub in the village.

Gamecock Barracks in Bramcote, near Nuneaton in Warwickshire, was the site of an out of use Royal Air Force station: a large, flat and grassed area with hangars, a runway and a collection of quarters for officers and non-commissioned ranks. Barracks accommodation for the young trainees was comfortable and the facilities offered good training, an education centre, gymnasium, chapel and swimming pool. We had little to complain about.

Life at Bramcote was busy, and a struggle. My monthly salary was about £200 for a family of three. Making ends meet – rental charges, food, petrol, heat and light and so on – was difficult. Later, Margaret Thatcher became Prime Minister and gave us a rapid, much-needed and welcome pay rise. It made life a little easier. But we still had to scrape and save for the basics. We had nothing left for anything else. That said, we enjoyed a happy life among our friends, especially Lieutenant John Keeling (another Geordie who became, with his family, a really good, trusted mate) and the other young officers, their wives and families.

Socially, plenty was going on with film nights, lunches and dinners in the Officers' Mess, built to a traditional Hore-Belisha style familiar at many RAF stations. As I awoke one morning after a particularly late and alcoholic dinner night, Jane gave me a stern look. "Where did you get that?" she asked accusingly, pointing at a big red bruise on my shoulder, looking remarkably like a love bite. I had no idea and couldn't account for it. Later, with me suffering from a hangover and sore shoulder and Jane not speaking to me much, we assembled in the Mess for brunch. The Commanding Officer came up to us and apologised for biting me. Telling him I had no idea what he was talking about, he explained to us both that, after dinner, we engaged in a game of Mess rugby where, with the room cleared and sofas upturned, two teams (the CO and senior officers versus troop commanders) stood at the tunnel entrance and fought their way from one end to the other. The first to get through would win and the losers would buy the champagne. The CO explained that, finding someone lying on top of him and blocking his airway, his only solution to avoid suffocation was to bite his way out. It worked, he survived and Jane was reassured that I had not misbehaved. I was relieved but it taught me that she kept her eye on me and behaving badly would not be a good idea.

Leading up to our first summer leave, John Keeling told me that he had secured a cheap flight through the RAF's indulgence scheme. For about £10, he could fly to the United States and, providing he could pay and the aircraft was available, he could fly on and get the return flight. Worried that he might have run out of cash by the time it came to the flight home, we agreed that he would leave his sports car with me and I would sell it and transfer the funds to him. I would work out how to do that and he would get back in time for the next term. Simple. But no. Keeling got across the States (despite being almost killed in an attempted knife robbery) and he wanted to contact me before he was completely broke and tell me to sell the car but he couldn't remember my number. Solution? Ring the Mess and get a message to me. He spent ages trying to get through and, almost down to his last few cents, the phone was at last picked up by Ying, our loyal and hardworking Chinese Mess waitress, whose English was not at all good.

"Arro?"

"Ying!" he shouted, relieved that he had finally got through. "It's me. Keeling."

"No," she shouted back. "Keeling in America. Bye." And she hung up. Keeling was broke, cursing and stranded but, by sheer good fortune, the RAF were at the airport ready and waiting to evacuate a casualty flying in from Belize. Keeling got his lift home. He had a lucky escape and he kept the car.

We continued our winter training programme and, as December approached, thoughts turned to leave after the Chapel Carol Service. All the Junior Leaders, instructors and staff assembled for the morning rehearsal of lessons and carols. Soon after it began, the padre stopped the organ.

"Is there any chance of you lot singing today?" he asked. "Let's try again."

And, moments later:

"Stop!"

Clearly unimpressed, he moved into the centre aisle and looked around the recruits.

"Fine. We'll try something else. We will pretend that every one of you in this half of the group is a Liverpool supporter and everyone on the other side supports Everton. This is the FA cup final, it's a grudge match and the score is one-all. There are three minutes to go, so when we get to the chorus, I want you to SING as if you want your team to WIN! All clear? Let's do it again."

He got exactly the result he was looking for. The chorus of

Noel, Noel got louder with each verse as the Juniors, all nerves gone, tried to outdo the other side. The noise could be heard throughout the Barracks. It was a good service in the end, delivered with the right spirit.

As we moved into my second year, I embarked on a new and challenging project during summer leave. The plan was to take a group of sixteen volunteers from Gothenburg, Sweden by train into the Arctic Circle and, from its start point on the Kvikjokk trail, walk about 240 miles in time to meet the train back to catch the ferry home. Volunteers, all Juniors, were easy to find and we trained by walking Hadrian's Wall and stretches of the Pennine Way, learning teamwork, tented living and endurance. We suffered some injuries and complaints from the lads but, as summer leave arrived, we were ready. Arriving at Gothenburg, we trekked to the station and boarded the train; thirty-six hours later, we arrived at Narvik. The signs to the trail were just outside the station. Exercise Northern Lights had begun.

Each day, one of our Juniors was selected to lead the stage, plotting the route, the next camp site and the distance to cover, which averaged about twelve miles. The trail was marked by cairns on the hilltops and the going varied according to the seasons. Winter would have made the trip much more difficult. In summer, for us, it was quite easy walking and we met our target times easily, finding a place to camp beside an (ice cold) stream each night. Waking up was more challenging, until I discovered a trick: shouting out the seconds taken to emerge from the bivouac earned each Junior the equivalent time with their heads in the stream. Getting up became easier!

Every third day or thereabouts, we reached a remote Lapp settlement to buy food and other stores. The prices were very high indeed. This was bad news. We had not been given enough to live on so, as the days passed, we resorted to rationing. The volunteers never complained, but the distances covered each day started to drop off; the lads were tired and the lack of food was a factor. As we neared the end we needed a very early start to meet the train and make the return journey. Fortunately – and with a strong pace-setter – we got there, luckily without injury, and set off for the coast. The lads were happy to get aboard the ferry.

We reached Nuneaton safely, in time to enjoy the rest of our leave. Jane was there to meet me at the station – a long-awaited sight! We felt we had done well, my post-exercise report was well received and we were refunded our claim for expenses. I would have preferred to get it before we left, so the lads would benefit when they needed it, but lesson learned! No Northern Lights though. You can't have everything.

Our return from leave was as busy as ever and, as we moved into the winter term, we had some good news. The annual Champion Troop Competition – a mix of military skills tests, fitness and inspections over two days – was won by Ironside Troop. My lads learned how good it felt to train and win. Finally, the Commanding Officer, another strong, good leader, informed me that I was to be posted to join 3rd Regiment, Royal Horse Artillery (3 RHA) based then in Devizes, but moving soon to Germany. This came as a surprise but was not unwelcome news; we would be living in Germany again and I was going to join a prestigious organisation, recognised for its standards of excellence, love of sport and admired by many for its performance. My car by this time was worn out (we couldn't afford the petrol, let alone the repairs, and it was threatening to break down at any moment), so I trekked off to a car dealer, arranged for a loan and got a replacement that would get us to Germany safely.

Two years leading a bunch of young Junior Leader Gunners at Bramcote taught me a lot about preparing these boys for adult Service. They arrived as immature, unfit and mostly unmotivated lads who had not experienced military discipline or learned respect for authority. Few had any interest in education and did not want to learn. They wanted to get on with it. Many joined to get away from a troubled home life with complicated family structures. They needed to be moulded into a team and learn the joy and pride to be felt from being successful. Getting them to that condition took time but, with patience and a good team of instructors supervising and advising, my troop began to grow in confidence and, come the end of the year, those that remained were certainly good enough to join their Regiments. I had got to know them well over the year and enjoyed watching their progress. The best went on to achieve high rank and be commissioned themselves. These were good lessons for later on.

On my arrival in 3 RHA in 1977, I was sent to J (Sidi Rezegh) Battery, named after a Young Officer, George Ward Gunn, who was awarded a posthumous Victoria Cross at Sidi Rezegh in the desert in WW2. My Battery Commander, Major Boxall Hunt, sent me ahead of the bulk of the soldiers and families to find accommodation. Without somewhere to go, they couldn't move at all, so the pressure was on to find something for the families. On arrival, I was told by the Headquarters staff that there were no quarters available but got agreement that anything I did find would be allocated to my people on a priority basis (I don't think the staff believed that I would find anything at all).

My German was very basic so, grabbing an interpreter, we set off on a search. Sometime later, we came across a pretty town near Paderborn called Bad Lippspringe; it had two large, high rise blocks of flats. I met the landlord and, *auf schlechte Deutsch*, explained that I was a soldier from England looking for several family apartments on a long-term lease, probably ten years at least. He smiled and said he had plenty to rent – help yourself. He even offered us the penthouse – no charge! He had everything we needed in excellent condition and I reserved the whole lot until I could confirm the numbers. I returned to the

Headquarters that afternoon and asked them to allocate the necessary apartments immediately. The staff were incredulous but, true to their word, actioned the paperwork. The families started to move in. When I left the Battery in 1980, most of them were still there living happily.

J Battery was equipped with the Swingfire anti-tank missile system, as were the other Batteries of 3 RHA but in independent, cold war roles and tasks. Each Battery was given administrative support by its affiliated Artillery Regiment; ours was 25 Field Regiment, based in Barker Barracks Paderborn and relationships between Regiment and Battery could be tricky as one tried to outdo the other. Sports competitions were a very bruising affair. It required patience and I would delight in showing just a little more polish and style than the other Batteries in the Regiment. The RHA wears the Cypher as its cap badge, characterised by the red backing to mark the achievements of Ward Gunn VC; 3 RHA strove to maintain its 'Tradition of Excellence' and our non-commissioned officers and soldiers held and protected our standards.

My troop of twenty Gunners was equipped with six missile launchers and they were a difficult bunch to command, proving to be unreliable and often frustratingly lacking in discipline. It required a good Troop Sergeant to maintain order, run the training programme and keep the vehicles well maintained. Our vehicles had missile simulators on board and we practised the firing sequence frequently as we prepared to deploy on firing camp with some good performances. Controlling a wire-guided missile, flying at high speed over 4,000 metres and subject to cross winds and heat haze, was not easy.

During autumn, as each major exercise ended and we returned to Barracks, our affiliated Regiment began a period of 'admin' when the equipment was cleaned and inspected, the stores and records checked and accommodation blocks prepared for the coming year. It was hard work and my Battery was determined to produce to a high standard; it was a clear demonstration of what the RHA reputation stood for. It was a busy period and we had little time for distractions. During the preparations, the Battery Captain, our Second in Command, called me in. He told me that he had to go away for the weekend and wanted me to prepare the Battery account for audit later that week. The books and financial records were all there and just needed tidying up and submitting the papers to the auditors. "Simple task," he said.

He was bluffing. I took the books home. The accounts were all there, the holdings of cash and in the bank account were correct but I could not resolve a major imbalance or account for the missing 200 Deutchmarks in the supporting papers. I worked late into the night, and during the next day, and finally found the error. The NAAFI supplied us with beer barrels for the Battery Bar called containers and expected us to prove that we still held them, or pay for the loss. Going through the invoices one by one and checking how the containers were recorded, I finally found the error. The missing 200 DM had been recorded against 'Funeral Expenses'. I corrected the error and was fuming at what the 2IC had done. Failing to tell me about the problem was bad enough but to cover it up by recording the figures against a soldier in the Battery who had taken his own life earlier that year was callous and dreadful. On his return, I discovered that he did not even have to be away and was just visiting friends. He had plenty of time to finish his accounts and solve the error himself. His idleness and complacency were thoroughly unprofessional. Since joining the Battery, I had never liked the 2IC and I resolved then never to trust him again.

Life in the Battery continued at its busy but enjoyable pace. Colin Boxall-Hunt was replaced by Major Nigel Richards. We had notable sporting successes, where I became good friends with Gunner Simeon 'Benny' Benoit, a highly talented rugby player from Domenica, and others in my troop. Jane made her own friends – in particular, our neighbour Avril Mitchell and her two daughters. Her daughter Becky and our son Brendan were inseparable; they spent many days getting up to mischief in each other's flats, including one memorable occasion when they redecorated several rooms with talcum powder. Our daughter, Katherine (she later chose Kate), was born in the British Military Hospital at Rinteln, in September 1978 and Jane was allowed home rather quicker than I thought would happen.

That summer led to my taking my troop back to Canada for the second time to provide the artillery, engineer, communications and logistic support for a Cavalry Regiment on its major exercise. My experience having been there before gave me a head start because I was familiar with the terrain and knew how the exercise would probably be carried out. My enthusiasm was soon to be dampened, however, because the Regiment involved were extremely unwelcoming and depressingly bored by the fact that they were there at all. Their performance was unprofessional, the standards were poor and my soldiers were not at all looked after. Over the three weeks, we got very little satisfaction from what was asked of us. In short, it was a thoroughly disappointing experience, not helped by the arrogance of some of the personalities involved. Fortunately, we departed on a period of Rest and Recuperation (which was aimed to give the exercising troops the time to relax after a demanding training period) and I went with three friends on a tour of the United States, visiting Wyoming and Montana and seeing Yellowstone Park.

Arriving at the small town of Cody, our stay coincided with the annual rodeo tournament and its typical Wild West feel (without the guns): horses and cowboys everywhere and a large saloon called The Golden Boot just across from our hotel. We felt completely out of place and gingerly entered the saloon, not knowing what to expect from a roomful of cowboys, a large bar and a Country and Western Band playing. We sat quietly in the corner over our beers and, gradually, the punters came across to see who we were. We ended up having a thoroughly good time and, with two days of our break to go, decided to stay in Cody. At the end, we became the talk of the town and were treated really well. We even talked about leaving the Army, moving out to the States and setting up a business there with our families. Even the bank manager was enthusiastic. But, as we drove back to our base at the end of our trip, the romance of the idea began to cool off and the reality set in. My time on R and R more than made up for a bad deployment to Canada. I knew then that I was right to join the Gunners and stay away from the Cavalry. As for our dream, we returned to our barracks and we did nothing about it, but one of our friends, Gerry Akhurst, fell in love with Cody and, some years later, went back to see the place. It hadn't changed much, he told us.

I enjoyed life in the Battery and we made lifelong friends. Returning from Canada and after another short spell in charge of a new troop – a much better bunch than my last one – I then took up the post of Battery Captain, the BC's second in command. I was responsible for running the troops' day-to-day activities, maintaining their vehicle and training programmes and social life. Fortunately, our new Battery bar, built by a gang of British housebuilders, proved to be a great success and we soon recovered the costs of the new bar and disco. Our Battery Sergeant Major Mick Whitham played a big part in this project. Mick and his lovely wife, Wendy, stayed in touch with us after our time in the Battery and we meet at our regular Regimental reunions. They are good people.

Our sport and social life continued and, as 1998 approached, I faced a big test: the Staff College exam. This was a big deal for me because passing the staff exam meant a possible selection to attend the staff course and was something to which we all aspired. Selection to attend the Staff College meant that we captains and junior majors were seen to be in the top 10% of the Army peer group and had the potential to fulfil key command and desk appointments in operational headquarters and in the Ministry of Defence (MOD). The potential to reach the highest ranks was there. It meant a great deal of study to prepare for two papers on strategic studies and a second, military technology paper. On the day, we assembled in a large room with about thirty of us and were handed the first paper requiring us to answer four exam questions in two and a half hours, roughly thirty minutes per paper. After a short break, we completed the second paper under the same rules. It was a hard day and required us to show the ability to answer the question by thinking logically and expressing arguments well. At the end, I felt I had been tested, had no idea how I had done but, as time progressed, I began to feel that perhaps it hadn't gone too badly and my research might have paid off. When the results were made public, my Commanding Officer rang me and said that he was delighted to tell me that I had passed – and passed quite easily – and that I would be recommended for a place at the Staff College.

This led to my next posting; I received a letter from Lieutenant General Tim Morony, soon to become Vice Chief of the General Staff and Second in Command of the Army, inviting me to work at the Ministry of Defence in London as his Assistant Military Assistant (AMA). Major Nigel Richards had served in the MOD before and was very excited by the letter. He said I must accept, so I did. That experience was to give me lessons about the Army that I will never forget.

My final task before I left J Battery was to go through vetting. The new job required that I be awarded 'Developed Vetting', allowing me access to the highest possible sensitive material –

Top Secret. It is a complicated business and can take months, as the authorities were very keen to prevent anyone from spying, or being vulnerable to disclosing secret information to terrorists or others determined to undermine the UK, rather like a John Le Carré novel. The guy chosen to interview me arrived late for his appointment and was in a hurry to get the job done. Working our way through the forms, my own background was easy; I came from a Devon farming family and had no concerns. Jane's was a different story. I was asked:

"Where does her father come from?"

"He's Irish. He was once a journalist."

"And her mother?"

"She comes from Sicily and has connections in New York. She died before we were married."

"And where did they get married?"

"Shanghai, China. Her father was working there."

"Does your wife have any siblings?"

Yes. Ten. All boys. I only know six of them and have no idea where the rest are. South Africa possibly, and one in jail, maybe."

He looked depressed but said little, probably because of the nightmare I'd just given him (possible connections with the IRA? China? Communism? The Mafia?). But thankfully, my vetting came through in a matter of weeks and I was able to return to the UK and prepare for the MOD.

I left J Battery in 1980 for London and the MOD, with some good memories and great friends whom I would see again, particularly Bob Harmes and Mick Whitham. I had been given my first taste of what it means to be a Horse Gunner and wanted more of it.

INTRODUCING HARRY

We returned to the UK and settled in to our new quarter, a small house in Kingston-upon-Thames and a short walk to the station, which was to become very familiar thanks to my daily commute to Waterloo.

On one of my first days at work, Field Marshal Sir Edwin 'Dwin' Bamall, the Chief of the General Staff (CGS) and Head of the Army, walked into my new office on the sixth floor of the MOD. His Military Assistant (MA), Mike Wilkes, a former Commanding Officer of 22 SAS (a big and imposing man, well worth keeping happy), said:

"CGS, can I introduce Captain Freddie Viggers, the new AMA?"

"Good morning, Harry," he said. "Welcome. You will like it here."

Lesson One: never correct a very senior officer, particularly when he is hard of hearing. "Thank you, CGS," I said rather nervously, hoping he wouldn't ask me anything difficult. He left. I looked at the MA. "That's it," Mike said, "from now on, your name is Harry, OK?" And so it was.

Among his many fine qualities, we soon discovered that Dwin was forgetful. A busy man, he would frequently misplace his favourite gold pen. It was a gift from a Middle Eastern VIP and, as was the tradition for the CGS of the time, filled with green ink – the standard Army colour. As he left the office for a lunch meeting, and usually in a rush, he would ring me from his car phone and shout:

"Harry! Lost the pen. Find the pen. I'll be back at two. Bye."

This would often leave me and Jeremy Knight the ADC (Aide De Camp) a very short space of time in which to find the pen and it would turn up in the strangest of places – in one of his trays, under the desk, fallen into the sofa, behind the toilet. Furniture was often taken out into the corridor during our search but it was always there when he got back.

The MOD is a bewildering place. Built on the site of the huge Whitehall Palace, where only King Henry VIII's wine cellar remains, it is a maze of corridors over six floors, crammed with offices full of busy people. Easy to get lost. Its layout is quite logical but it still took me about three months to begin to grasp it and know how to find people in a hurry. Understanding how the place worked and linked in to other functions of government business, particularly the Foreign Office and Treasury, and the role of senior politicians, took even longer. My boss, General Tim Morony, could not have been better to work for – calm, patient, a great sense of humour and always ready to explain to me what was happening. His wife, Sally, was also a great help and we enjoyed getting to know their boys, Michael and Matthew. Once, when their parents were away, his two boys were given the General's flat. They'd planned to be there until Tuesday, when the General was due to return, but on Monday, the General rang to say he'd be returning a day early and he required a car to collect him from the station. I went round to the flat and walked in to find it in a complete state. "Lads," I said, "your father will be back at 6pm." The boys moved like a whirlwind.

During the course of a typical working day I saw important people going about their business – the Secretary of State for Defence and his Junior Ministers, the Chief of the Defence Staff and Heads of the Navy and RAF, other senior officers and civil servants. It was heady stuff. My role as AMA was to look after my General: to arrange his daily programme, prepare his papers, meet and greet his visitors and escort them from the building after their meeting was over, and to take his phone calls. My direct boss when I arrived was Colonel John Parkes, a former Gurkha Officer, who liked his coffee in the morning.

As part of my handover, John said that I needed to understand how the phone worked. I looked puzzled and he explained that my phone and the MA's had different switches to isolate the microphone. Mine allowed me to listen in on conversations and take notes without being heard if I coughed or sneezed and the switch had to be pushed down, while the phone belonging to my boss, John Parkes, needed to be pushed up. This was important because, on one occasion, one Field Marshal rang to give advice to the Vice Chief and the MA had to listen in because conversations could be quite lengthy and detailed. Apparently, the Field Marshal did this quite regularly and had a reputation for being very direct and impatient. On one occasion, John Parkes took the Field Marshal's call on my phone and transferred him to General Stanier. Thinking he had isolated the microphone correctly in the off position, he said to the other officers in the room:

"Crickey. You should listen to this. He's giving the Vice Chief a real wigging."

The conversation stopped. There was silence then a cough. Parkes realised what he had done.

"Excuse me, Field Marshal," said the Vice Chief. The door

to his office crashed open and he came in red faced and looking very angry.

"We can do without your bloody asides, MA," shouted the General and he stormed back to finish his conversation with the Field Marshal.

Fortunately, John survived this incident (and, perhaps, the sack) but the experience clearly had a big impact on him and explained why he was so concerned that I should know the drill. I didn't forget and reminded myself of the procedure every morning.

John Parkes was later replaced by Colonel Tony Piggott, a Royal Engineer Officer, who was equally good and an excellent MA and very helpful to work for. I was lucky to have such able people around me. The office staff supporting us were the same. Tony was later to marry Felicity and we have stayed in touch.

Perhaps my most important task was to sit in on meetings and record the key parts of the discussions taking place between these great men. I learned the art of note-taking very quickly. Often, after a meeting or phone call, General Tim or other officers would come into my office and ask, "What did I agree to? What did I say? What did he say?"

In my first year, I watched the then Secretary of State take his axe to the Royal Navy to make savings (in other words, cuts). The Civil Service held the whip hand here and began to revel in their role and relationship with the military. This made us all feel uncomfortable as, despite the advice of the Senior Officers of the Navy, real reductions in capability were being proposed and actioned.

It was a difficult first year, punctuated by three tense incidents.

Police Constable Trevor Lock was having a quiet time, guarding the Iranian Embassy in central London, when armed terrorists stormed the building, moved upstairs and took hostages. Trevor was among them. As the situation developed with the police in the lead, a group from the SAS counter terrorist unit moved quietly to a site in London and began to prepare to enter the Embassy and recover the hostages, should the order be given. Negotiations for hostage release and rehearsals carried on over several days until, eventually, the terrorists shot and killed a hostage. This was enough; the Police Commander passed control to the SAS and, minutes later, the assault began in full view of the media. CGS, by chance, was at home and watching TV. He rang his MA and gave him a running commentary as troopers, armed, dressed in black and wearing respirators, abseiled from the roof of the building to the balconies below. CGS was getting more and more excited and the MA's frustration was obvious; he had trained his men to do exactly this kind of thing and felt he should have been there.

Loud explosions took out the windows and the assault team entered the room, except for one who was caught up in the fire and fell from the rope. Shots and more explosions rang out. We watched the TV in the office, transfixed, until we heard that the terrorists, bar one, were dead and the hostages were safe. To our surprise and through all the days of the siege, PC Trevor Lock kept his pistol concealed from the terrorists. His courage was exceptional. There was relief all round as, among the beer, fags and TV replays, Margaret Thatcher went to meet the SAS squadron to thank them. The soldiers were heroes but they moved back to their home base and stayed anonymous. The legend of the SAS had been enhanced beyond measure and their motto – Who Dares Wins – was there for all to see. I admired them for it, not knowing then that, although I was never really tempted to have a go at the gruelling selection tests, I would have quite a lot to do with the SAS in the future. They are genuinely extraordinary people.

As we entered my second year, I continued with my other

morning duty, which was to sift through the bulk of highly classified Diplomatic Telegrams (DIPTELS) to see which ones may be of interest to my boss and which I could destroy. It sounds more interesting than it was. On one day, a short, innocuous DIPTEL arrived, which reported that a bunch of scrap metal dealers had arrived at a dock in South Georgia. I threw it in the out tray – General Tim need not see it. Then, for some reason, I thought he might be amused by it and so I recovered it. Thankfully. Because suddenly CGS's MA rushed into the room, shouting "Where's the f'ing DIPTEL? The one about South Georgia?" I pulled it from the General's in-tray, Mike grabbed it from me and moved quickly into CGS's office. Several senior officers came and went and Mike emerged some time later in a much better mood. Argentina's invasion of the Falkland Islands had begun; the scrap metal dealers mentioned in the DIPTEL were in fact covert Argentinian Forces.

From then on, the mood at work changed. Prime Minister Thatcher was determined and unswerving; our territory had been seized and we would get it back, by force if necessary. No questions. This time, the military took the lead and the Civil Service were mere bystanders. I was re-assured that, when it really mattered, people knew their place. The Secretary of State's game with the Navy had failed.

Frantic preparations continued and the task force sailed while diplomacy was underway. We had several difficult times and issues to manage: the battle for Goose Green; the air attack on the Galahad at Bluff Cove that killed and maimed the soldiers of the Welsh Guards, including the badly injured Simon Weston; the sinking of the Belgrano; the advance to Port Stanley, the battle and the eventual surrender. It was a victory that underpinned and characterised much of the Thatcher legacy. She was not always a popular leader but she was undeniably a formidable woman with a strong set of personal values.

The third incident occurred on 20th July 1982. At around midday, the windows of our office in the MOD shook and we heard a loud explosion. The IRA had detonated a massive bomb on South Carriage Drive in Hyde Park. The bomb was exploded remotely as the Queen's Life Guard was riding towards Whitehall for the morning ceremony of guard mounting and its impact shook us all. In total, an officer and three men of the Blues and Royals were killed and seven horses also died. The scene was televised and the effect was horrific to watch. Shortly after that, another bomb exploded under the band stand in Regent's Park while the Band of the Royal Green Jackets entertained the public. Seven bandsmen died. Attention soon turned to a horse called Sefton, which was badly injured in Hyde Park. This horse became a symbol of national determination that these terrorists would not succeed and we received regular updates of his progress. The squadron commander, Major Anthony de Ritter, answered hundreds if not thousands of letters and good will messages. I was to meet Anthony again on my next tour at the Staff College; he was a fine officer with a delightful sense of humour and fun to be around. Sefton survived and became famous as he was made Horse of the Year. The police arrested, jailed and later released those believed to be responsible but, so far, no-one has been found guilty of this callous attack. I somehow doubt that, given the passage of time, anybody now will be. The Army lost some good men that day.

On the family front, we were busy. We managed to link up with Gil and Twink Bray, who by then were living nearby in Thames Ditton, and discovered our love of bridge. We played at each other's houses, often into the early hours of the morning, chatting and enjoying lots of wine. We didn't keep score. Around this time, their son, Matthew, arrived and a few years later, a daughter, Natasha. Jane became her godmother.

Soon, the time came for me to move on from the MOD. I had

been awarded a place at the Army Staff College in Camberley and a short, technical course at Shrivenham. We had been given a quarter near the college but we decided to stay at Kingston until I was ready to move. I left the MOD with lessons and memories that would serve me well in the years ahead, confident that my time at the Staff College would not be wasted.

I had learned a lot about the workings of the MOD in my two years there. At a time of significant budgetary pressure, I witnessed senior officers working under real pressure to preserve military capability where the threat posed by the Cold War internationally was often downplayed. Here, Ministers and the Civil Service were in the van of the debate. The Falklands crisis, however, changed that dynamic. Now the military took the lead as the Royal Navy and other Services set off in a hurry to liberate the islands as directed by Prime Minister Thatcher. Risks were taken and, through a mix of grit, determination and no little courage, victory was achieved. It was a salutary historical lesson. Meanwhile, the threat posed by global and Irish terrorism continued and the Army could not take its eye off the ball. Personally, I enjoyed the demands of the job and seeing these great men at work. I had a marvellous boss in General Sir Tim Morony, who had immense humility and taught me a great deal.

BACK TO SCHOOL

The tutor at The Royal Military College of Science Shrivenham entered the theatre on Friday afternoon to give us a lecture on ballistics or something equally esoteric. It had been a long week and the weekend beckoned. He was carrying a bunch of visual aids, known to us as vufoils, which were each the size of a house brick. As he spoke, he began to put his vufoils on the screen above our heads, one by one, and described them in a tone guaranteed to put even the keenest to sleep. Thirty minutes into his pitch, a voice from the top tier came: "This is outrageous." He rose and left the theatre. "Quite," said another, and he left too. A lesson in how not to prepare and present, courtesy of a speaker who quite obviously was too lazy to organise, rehearse and deliver his content in an engaging or effective way.

Our time on the Shrivenham course followed this pattern and proved to me that I was not cut out to follow a technical career. I had little interest in that side of life but my time in the MOD did allow me to see how technology and the 'appliance of science' could benefit the Army in the future. I came away without a recommendation for future postings that needed a technical background. Mission accomplished then! But, as the course ended, we knew that those selected for formal staff training were in the top 10% of the Army, so we couldn't be that bad.

As the course at Shrivenham lasted three months, we moved house to Camberley. When Brendan turned eight, and after many changes of school, we turned our minds to his long term future and private education. A friend recommended Sherborne Prep School in Dorset. We had no experience of the boarding scheme and, in hindsight, I think we should have shopped around to ensure we found the best fit for our son. We picked Sherborne and, as the date arrived, we took him to the school and helped him settle in with his clothes and tuck box. Driving home was really hard; we had said goodbye to our little boy knowing that, according to the rules, we could write to him but would not hear his voice again for weeks. Had we done the right thing? Should we turn round and bring him home? Many military parents will know what we were feeling. It was tempting to go back but we felt that continuing on would be better for our son in the long term and, although difficult, we should see it through. The house was quiet without him; his sister missed him a lot. Jane wrote to Brendan every day and, soon, we got a reply telling us what he had done. He sounded OK! A phone call later would reinforce that and we counted the days until we could go to collect him for his holiday.

The Staff College at Camberley was divided into three divisions and classes, each of ten students with a range of Army experiences. The Commandant, Major General John Akehurst, had come recently from commanding an armoured division in Germany and, soon before that, in command of fighting troops in the Dhofar Campaign in the Middle East. He had written a book about his exploits called *We won a War*, which prompted someone with a sense of humour to show the book cover on the screen in the main lecture theatre at the start of each presentation. The title read, 'What do you think of it Dhofar?' We hoped the slide would be taken off before the Commandant walked in. Most times, it was. But John was a great example and he would have seen the joke if we had been caught winding him up.

The Staff College year was hard work. Always under the watchful eye of the directing staff, the course consisted of a series of subject areas of military interest based on the Cold War, the workings of the MOD, presentations by keynote speakers and discussions. We were under constant assessment; each term centred on written tests, delivered and marked against the clock. I found some of these easier than others but generally came away with a satisfactory grade.

The programme also included a series of visits to see how our own and other nations' Service organisations operated. A trip to RAF Coltishall gave me a superb flight in a Jaguar aircraft (the only time I ever won a worthwhile raffle prize) to experience a high speed, gut-squeezing flight over The Wash at low level to conduct a simulated attack in the Lake District. Abroad, I missed a group visit to the French navy where, after an impressive demonstration by a fully-dressed diver, the visit concluded with a delicious French dinner. I heard later that the group leader rose to thank his hosts for a wonderful and informative experience. His French accent was not at all good and difficult to follow for both Brits and the French. Holding back the tears of laughter was even harder when the leader got to the diver bit and thanked them for showing him the "plongeur formidable." The Brits knew what he meant but I'm not sure the French did.

Our tour of Europe took in visits to NATO, the EU in Brussels (where too many litres of lager and trays of garlic-filled *moules* were a test for any constitution), the British Army in

Germany and Berlin. 1983 in Berlin was the time of the Cold War and we were under strict instructions to behave and cause no offence to the East Germans, who clearly knew about our visit and were watching us very carefully. Tom Hanks's film *Bridge of Spies*, directed by Stephen Spielberg, captures the mood perfectly. Going to the Berlin Wall to see Checkpoint Charlie and observing the guards looking at us from the high towers (and probably photographing us too) was a sobering experience, made all the more so after a visit to the museum to see examples of what downtrodden people had done to try to escape, including microlight aircraft, false car boots, fake passes and uniforms. They were desperate to get away and many failed, or even died in the attempt. Returning from Berlin by train was also fascinating as we left the grey skies, factories and apartments of the German Democratic Republic, past the Regiments of tanks lined up in the barracks of Magdeburg with barrels all facing west. Entering West Germany, where everything changed to colour, was a different world and we were glad to back again.

Socially, life was fun. As students, we lived in quarters of varying standards and builds; ours were known as the railway carriages and there were others allocated to the overseas students. One family from the Middle East managed to live in one quarter with twelve of his thirteen children. We students enjoyed our sport and made the most of the facilities. Our rugby team only had one victory against our American counterparts in Frankfurt but we entertained well. The rugby squad and their wives were a great bunch. Jane and I had a hilarious bike ride home in the early hours after a typically good disco evening; I'll never know how we didn't get lost in the woods or fall off and injure ourselves.

As the year progressed, our minds turned to next steps. Most of the students would go on to Staff (Desk) appointments, while a few would be sent to Regimental Duty. As the day of publication neared, speculation grew as the students began to see who were the likely 'stars' and would go on to the top jobs with greatest potential. I was relaxed because, at the 3 RHA Reunion Dinner the year before, I was asked by the Commanding Officer, Lieutenant Colonel Graham Hollands, whom I had met on my first tour with J Battery, if I would like to return to his Regiment as the Battery Commander of J (Sidi Rezegh) Battery. What a great question! Graham was a marvellous officer – relaxed, professional and highly competitive – exactly the qualities I admired in a future boss. I knew he would look after my soldiers and give us a fantastic tour. Yes please!

So all I needed to do was await the day of the announcement and not give too much away – plans have a nasty habit of changing. Others had a more memorable time. As we entered our syndicate rooms, in came an impressive officer of the Grenadier Guards. Gerald was an able man, tall and well versed in the social life of London. He was also a high quality, first-class rugby player. He was looking solemn and was wearing his forage cap. At that time early in the morning, the convention was that no-one spoke to a Guards Officer until he had taken his cap off. He sat down and began to open his envelope as all the students in the room did. Silence, broken only by Gerald: "Tell me, someone: where the f*** is Catterick?" He had got a top job in a Brigade Headquarters but he did manage a smile as we laughed at him. My future was confirmed; Major Viggers was returning to 3 RHA to command J Battery. I could not have wished for more. Jane was happy too – we had good memories of the soldiers and their wives from our last tour with them.

The end of our year brought about revues, pantomimes and our final exercise, designed to bring together the skills we had learned thus far. The exercise was set in a Cold War scenario, with the Red team (the Warsaw Pact) advancing against the Blue Team (NATO forces from Europe and the US). In our scenario,

Red had invaded the south coast and was advancing north. Students were given command appointments and I was made the General Officer Commanding of an armoured division, tasked with defending Hampshire on the Winchester-Newbury Road. There then followed days of pretty frantic planning, issuing orders and preparations, all based around large maps, unit designators and symbols.

On day one of the three-day exercise, the game began. Our plan was to lure the Red Force into the desired ambush site near Beacon Hill and engage the enemy with everything at our disposal. I only hoped someone had told Lord Carnarvon resting in peace in his tomb on top of the hill! To our pleasure, the plan began to work. The enemy behaved as predicted and soon presented the ideal target array. The time was right but nothing happened. No overwhelming firepower from guns and aircraft, nothing. Red Force moved on. I was getting more and more frustrated; had my plan started to unravel? Had we lost? Major Hamish Fletcher, a robust, physically imposing paratrooper, was playing the role of my Chief of Staff. Sensing my annoyance, he said, "Leave it with me," and walked out. Shortly afterwards, things started to happen, weapons were fired and targets started to disappear from the map. Hamish returned.

"Where have you been?"
"I've been to speak to him."
"Who?"
"The guy responsible for triggering our ambush as the enemy moved into the chosen area."
"And?"
"I told him to get a grip. Then I punched him. Hard."
"Is he OK?"
"He's switched on now. He'll get over it."

The exercise ended soon after that and we had done it – and done well. The Red Team was deemed to have been beaten back.

We were tired but felt we had acquitted ourselves well. Soon after that, our year at the Staff College ended and we left for our pre-deployment courses and new appointments. My time at the Staff College was an excellent experience. It brought together the things I had learned up to that point and gave me a good understanding of the workings of the MOD and operational planning in the Cold War context. I had made some good friends, who I knew would always be ready to help if I ever needed it.

As my mind turned its focus to Germany and 3 RHA, I knew that I was heading for a challenging but fun time with some first class soldiers. I was not disappointed.

GERMANY, CANADA, NORTHERN LIGHTS: REVISITED

Our return to Paderborn to re-join 3rd Regiment, Royal Horse Artillery in 1984 was straightforward. There were some high quality officers and soldiers there and Lieutenant Colonel Graham 'Lofty' Hollands was in command. 3 RHA was in the process of changing its roles, handing back the Swingfire anti-tank missile and taking over the 105mm Abbot artillery system from 25 Regiment. I knew this Regiment and its soldiers well from my last tour with J Battery and was familiar with how to operate the gun, thanks to my experiences learned during my first posting to 40 Regiment. I hadn't forgotten the skills needed and we planned on a range of training to develop my teams. Thankfully, my soldiers had the necessary trade qualifications and they also remembered the basic military skills. They weren't fit enough to embark on the Regiment's own programme, so we did a lot of physical training to rectify it.

As part of my settling in, Graham gave me two orders as Battery Commander of J (Sidi Rezegh) Battery: win the Gunner

Rugby Cup in Germany and look after our wives. The first was easy, I thought. We had a good squad of able players who wanted to win and I had the time to plan, train and prepare. The second was do-able, too, with Jane by my side. She was very popular after our first tour there. This was important, for the next two years were going to be a very busy time indeed, with a good deal of separation. The girls needed looking after while we men were away on exercise in Germany and, later, Canada.

As far as rugby was concerned, we knew we had the ability and talent to win but were in need of turning ourselves into a good team. We played regularly and, in 1984, we set off for a playing tour of the UK. Basing ourselves at my old Junior Leaders' barracks in Bramcote, we played two teams over three days, losing only to a particularly tough side from the Nuneaton Fire Service. It was hard fought but they deserved the win and we learned how we had to be fit enough to support each other. Socialising was definitely off limits and we decided to begin regular physical training and matches when we got back. Our final game was in London at Woolwich, the home of the Royal Artillery against Blackheath Rugby Club. We did not want to go out with a disappointing result so came away with a second win. Played three, won two was good enough for us and we were well set up for the final against 47 Regiment Royal Artillery in Dortmund on a wet and waterlogged pitch that called for a good deal of commitment and team spirit. We won the rugby cup (as ordered) and my team made the most of the victory.

My Battery also conducted a number of visits to our barracks and away from home. Major General Philip Tower also commanded J Battery and hd been the Commanding Officer of 3 RHA. He was best known as a CO for winning the Inter Services polo competition but I knew him as the Commandant of Sandhurst during my time as a cadet there. He came to spend two days with us and he thoroughly enjoyed meeting the soldiers. I took the trouble to explain who he was and what he had done so they enjoyed hearing his stories, particularly in the Sergeants' Mess, where he was never left without a full pint. It was a highly successful visit and I kept Philip informed of what we were up to.

I also had two famous battles to commemorate. As part of our young officers' training programme, the CO asked me to give a presentation about desert warfare in WW2. This was a good task for me as we had a connection with Sidi Rezegh in Libya that I knew about from my first tour with the Battery, where George Ward Gunn won a posthumous VC. I also knew that one of George's comrades at the battle was Brigadier Arthur Hardie MC and he agreed to visit the Regiment and give a talk to our officers about his experiences. He came with his son to spend a couple of days with the Battery. He stayed with us and the talk he gave was excellent, bringing to life how it was to live, fight and be killed in the heat and dust of the desert. Arthur sadly died some years later. We had kept in touch in the meantime. He was a good man.

My Battery had a further connection with Le Cateau in France, when three Victoria Crosses were won in a single action in 1914 as the guns were rescued under fire from the advancing German troops. The action is best remembered in a painting by Terence Cuneo called *Saving the guns at Le Cateau*. It shows the men riding away from the fire and is now displayed in our Regimental Officers' Mess. Cuneo is renowned for always including a mouse near the action somewhere in the battle in his paintings, and they can be difficult to spot. One of the men in the painting who was awarded the VC was Driver Fred Luke and, now in his 90s, he came to visit our Battery with his daughter. He was a fascinating, quiet and modest man who typically downplayed his role. Yet again, my sergeants and the soldiers entertained him royally and, thankfully, we got him home in one piece.

As 1984 was the 70th anniversary of the battle, the mayor and people of Le Cateau invited my Battery to visit the town to mark the occasion with a parade, march past, football game and celebration afterwards. We accepted and my Battery Sergeant Major, Gordon Cutter, set to with training the football team and the parade format. I scribbled a response and asked the Adjutant, a fluent French speaker, to translate it for me. With the speech ready, I asked the BSM for a status report. Like him, my boys came from the North East and were tough, uncompromising types from mining stock.

"The parade is ready. The football is rubbish. We're going to get hammered," he said. Time to worry.

We left for France and on our arrival received a very warm welcome from the French. I replied to the Mayor's welcome in French and the BSM was astonished at my accent, as were the soldiers on parade.

"Strewth BC! How did you do that?" the BSM asked afterwards.

"Easy when you know, BSM. Now, let's win the football."

We lost. Heavily. Fortunately, the party and reception went well with no bad behaviour and we got home with reputation intact and quickly forgot the football.

Living in Paderborn gave us good opportunities to travel around Germany and get back to the UK. Two trips were memorable. First was our journey to the Mohnesee Dam, made famous in the film *The Dambusters*. The film tells the story of Wing Commander Guy Gibson leading his squadron of Lancaster bombers to attack and destroy the industrial base along the Ruhr valley in May 1943. Looking out over the reservoir, the dam and its fortifications showed the remarkable skills and bravery of the pilots to position the aircraft accurately and under intense enemy fire to drop the bouncing bomb. The Mohne and Eder dams were hit successfully in the raid and only the Sorpe dam was hit above the waterline. It was a tremendously brave and audacious attack. In the 1960s, Barnes Wallis, the inventor of the bouncing bomb, came to tell his story to my school. It was good to see the effects of his innovative work and technical know-how some forty years later.

Our other trip, closer to Paderborn this time, was to walk around the renowned Schloss Wewelsburg. This was a cult building that Hitler envisaged would be the place from which the SS would govern his conquests after victory in WW2. It had a very dark and disturbing history, with stories of imprisonment and torture, and was not a place I would want to spend the night in. By the time we visited, it had become a tourist site, so the lessons of WW2 were still being remembered.

Back in barracks, our minds soon turned to training and my major event of the year – Canada.

I had been twice before, so knew a bit about the place.

We trained hard for it. Equipped with six 105mm and three 155mm self-propelled guns, my job was to fire in support of my affiliated Regiment, the Royal Scots Dragoon Guards, best known for their recording of *Amazing Grace* and, more recently, *Highland Cathedral*. I developed a real love of bagpipe music at around the same time as Jane invested in some earplugs. My commanding officer was Lieutenant Colonel Jonnie Hall. I liked him immediately and we have stayed in touch with him and his wife, Sarah. Jonnie was an outstanding CO and taught me a huge amount about command and leadership. I looked forward to and really enjoyed seeing Jonnie and his team in our work-up period and admired them for the interest they took in my soldiers and families. In many ways, I felt part of his Regimental family and talked to him whenever I needed advice. As a friend, he was always completely reliable and trustworthy. Professionally, he was just the same. I looked up to him as one of the most influential people as a CO with whom I ever served. After my last experience, it restored my faith in Cavalry Regiments as decent people.

My exercise programme had one fortunate but worrying incident. During a live firing mission, one of my large 155mm guns fired incorrectly. The round landed some distance away but was observed hitting the prairie in a safe place. Had it landed unsafely, my team calculated that it would almost certainly have caused serious casualties and perhaps even killed some Scots Dragoon soldiers. "Check Fire" was ordered immediately and the gun crews stopped what they were doing and touched nothing. We looked in detail at what happened, found the problem gun and informed the crew. The gun commander, a sergeant, agreed that this was an error in drill, rather than an error of drill, and was shocked when he was told about what could have happened. Nervously, I reported to Jonnie and explained what had happened. He said that he would let the exercise continue and would look at the incident later. We continued firing without incident and, as the exercise ended, Johnnie said that the Sergeant had clearly done well, learned his lesson and, as far as he was concerned, the issue was closed. I debriefed the man and said that no further action would be taken. Much to my surprise, I learned later that, on returning to his own barracks, his own CO took up the case again and disciplined him for the error. I was not involved nor consulted about the incident and I felt that the outcome was a great pity as I didn't think he deserved that. Luckily, it did no harm to our performance or reputation and I hope the man concerned soon got his career back on track.

Our trip to Canada went well and, without doubt, was the highlight of my year. I was tested and questioned but my boys rose to the challenge at every turn. Aside from the planned admin days, we were on the go all day and often into the night, firing all kinds of ammunition. On one particularly dark night and a long route march, the CO called us to a halt and we watched a stunning display of the Northern Lights. So, nearly ten years after leaving Bramcote and our Arctic walking adventure, I did eventually get to see what we went there for. Marvellous.

At the end of the exercise, I drove to the gun position on my way home to see my boys and thank them. One look in their eyes told me all I needed to know. They were exhausted and I realised that I had trained them too hard in the work-up period and asked too much of them in the exercise itself. This was a big lesson for me – you have to get the pace right. My boys didn't let me down and I owe them a lot for that.

We returned safely and got on with the end of year training. Shortly after the Canada exercise, we said goodbye to a young man with great leadership potential. Edward Billington joined J Battery on a six-month Short Service Limited Commission to see if a military career might appeal to him. I liked Ed immediately and my men did too. They adopted him from the start and taught him the basic artillery skills as we trained to go to Canada. He entered into all our activities with great enthusiasm and, once we got there, he had a very successful exercise. On our return, I said to the Commanding Officer that Ed didn't need to go to Sandhurst. He had all the skills and just needed experience; given the number of young men I had met on similar schemes, it was only the second time I had said that. (Ian Sinclair had joined us in 40 Regiment and had shown his talents then. I sang his praises to Peter Bonnet in a similar way). Sadly, Ed struggled with his future career on his return and eventually followed his family in the sugar industry. Jane and I visited the family home in the Wirral and were looked after very generously by his delightful parents. They explained that Ed was disappointed that he could not try for a commission but he needed to move on to complete university and learn new skills. It was a pity for the Gunners (although Ian Sinclair did eventually join the Regiment and went on to have a very successful career himself). We and Ed have stayed in occasional touch over the years and I've enjoyed hearing about his undoubted successes.

Returning from Canada was an anti-climax and nothing could replace our time there but, all too soon, the time came to move on. Lieutenant Colonel John Dean, my commanding officer, called me in: "Congratulations, Freddie, you are off to Tidworth to be Chief of Staff of 1st Infantry Brigade. Your boss is Brigadier John Wilsey. You will like him." I knew that this was a good tour to get, despite knowing nothing about Tidworth. It would turn out to be another testing time. As our tour closed, I thanked and said goodbye to so many good people – too many to mention – particularly my marvellous set of rugby players. They were happy days.

Looking back on my time as a Battery Commander, I felt that I had looked after my soldiers pretty well. My young junior non-commissioned officers had been stretched and their potential identified. The senior ones had also been set on good career paths with encouraging promotion prospects. I had fought for my men and, with the support of others, managed to help a couple struggling to become foster parents. David Tickner, my marvellous Padre, and I were able to prevent the social services placing a family on the 'At Risk' register. This would have been grossly unfair as there was no supporting evidence; it would take months to remove them from the list and they would face the very real threat of their children being take into care.

Dealing with and observing others outside my area, I also saw some disturbing personality characteristics in the Army. Those in command generally fell into two groups. The first took a real, genuine interest in and fought for their soldiers and their families. I referred to these as the 'downlookers'. The other group was made up of the more ambitious types who placed advancing their own careers above the needs of their people, regardless of the consequences. They are the 'uplookers'. The actions and motives of these two groups are easy to spot and the effects can be damaging. I knew the group I was in and sadly was to see much of the other group later in my career.

Jane had had a busy, sometimes stressful, but enjoyable two years as well. She looked after the Battery wives superbly while we were away and dealt with a number of difficult issues that always arise when the men are not at home: arguments, schoolchildren's behaviour, marriage issues, to name a few. She was held in great affection and, even now, many of the wives stay in touch with her at our reunions and parades. It feels like we were part of a big family with some great memories of genuinely good people.

FIRST INFANTRY BRIGADE

Leaving the Regiment again in 1985 to go to 1st Infantry Brigade, after two great years with J Battery, was a real wrench, but there were busy times ahead. We settled in to our new quarter in Tidworth Garrison and met our next door neighbours, Paddy and Annie George. Paddy was a determined, strong Royal Marine and we were to work very closely together and become really good friends from then on. Their three boys became sparring partners with Brendan immediately and they were to get into all sorts of scrapes at home and on holidays, usually with our daughter Kate acting as hostage (not voluntarily).

Headquarters of First Infantry Brigade in Tidworth stood within the grounds of former Victorian barracks with historic names from the days of Empire, including Aliwal, Jellalabad and Bhurtpore. Here, the men lived upstairs and the horses were stabled below in what were clearly fairly basic conditions. My offices were in the former maternity hospital where, I was told, I had a private ward. Often, visitors would arrive at our security gate to see the rooms where they had been born. Molly Rimmell, my PA, occupied the office opposite that we thought had once been used by the ward sister and, knowing what strict disciplinarians sisters could be, I thought that she was the perfect choice for the role. Nobody, including the Brigade Commander, messed with Molly.

First Brigade, commanded by Brigadier John Wilsey, was big and, at about 15,000 troops, almost the size of an Army division. Our role in the event of an invasion by the Warsaw Pact was to defend Schleswig Holstein in Northern Germany, or possibly Copenhagen in Denmark. This was do-or-die stuff, akin to Rorke's Drift at the time of the Zulu Wars. NATO would put up a valiant fight and, ultimately, be overrun in the attempt. But, by then, we would be in the middle of World War 3, so no-one would really know the outcome.

The brigade staff had well-developed plans should the order to deploy be given and we conducted a series of visits to plan the support we would get from our NATO allies. We were well looked after during our trips, particularly going to Denmark and visiting Copenhagen, the little mermaid on the docks and the royal porcelain collection. Our Danish allies usually put us up in the well-known Kastellet, often used as the home of the Danish royal family and a very short walk to the restaurants and shops. It is a very historic building and well worth a visit.

We took our task seriously and my job in the first year was to train and prepare the brigade for 'Bold Guard', its major multinational exercise in Germany with a German/Danish Army Force led by a highly impressive German Officer, General Henning Von Ondarza. He was a charming man whose desk was adorned by a photograph of General Erwin Rommel. Henning drew inspiration for battle planning from the Desert Fox's tactics in Africa in WW2. In our work-up training we tried to emulate that but soon discovered the spatial limitations of Salisbury Plain when trying to mobilise an entire brigade. This quickly and obviously became my 'trade test' when I would show John

Wilsey and his command team that I knew what I was doing. Thankfully, my Staff College training and the planning paid off and I was helped no end by having an 'enemy' opposition force from the Parachute Regiment, commanded by Lt Colonel Mike Jackson. Of him, I was to see much more later on. He was impressive then and the Paras did us proud. (I sometimes thought I should have tried to join them instead of the Gunners after Sandhurst – and was, in fact, invited to do so in my final term – but, knowing that I was brought up in Devon, John Wilsey could not believe that I did not join his own Regiment, The Devon and Dorsets. He often reminded me of that).

Our exercise in Germany, Bold Guard, went well but, by the end, I was exhausted. In a six day period, I had not slept for longer than two hours and had never been so tired. The effect was scary; I couldn't think quickly or focus on what I was doing, my speech was slurred and I hadn't eaten very much at all. Even John Wilsey saw that I was deteriorating badly and spoke to me about it. I was grateful that I smoked to keep going and the final phase of the exercise ended just in time, I collapsed onto my camp bed and slept all night. It was another big lesson for me – no-one is irreplaceable and I had to learn to delegate more. I had taken a big risk and I got away with it.

There were significant changes on the home front. We bought our first house in a pretty village called Winterslow near Salisbury and finally felt settled enough to own our first family dog, a rescue mongrel whom we called Max. The daily commute was compensated by living in the community and getting to know some good people; cricket matches on Sunday, captained by our friendly plumber, were fun times.

We returned to England and, soon after that, John left to join the Royal College of Defence Studies, to be replaced by Brigadier David Thomson, another highly likeable and talented officer with a reputation as a man with considerable operational experience, having served with the Argyll and Sutherland Highlanders in Aden, Germany and Northern Ireland. He too, was to become a good friend and excellent boss, a joy to work for.

1987 came with a further big event. The brigade was to support another major exercise involving the Army, Royal Navy and Royal Air Force in Scotland, called Purple Warrior.

Purple Warrior was based on an amphibious exercise area near Stranraer and an RAF station called West Freugh – not a particularly edifying place at the time – and a short helicopter flight to the island of Arran. Our task was to make the exercise run smoothly and efficiently and, as this was the most ambitious event in the military calendar to date, the eyes were on us all. It had to go well and we knew it but we were not helped by an exercise planning team who appeared disinterested, to say the least. David did his best to cheer us up but it was very hard work as the two exercising organisations, the Paras and the Marines, each tried to out-do the other. We had the Gurkhas there to get involved as an opposition force. When we found one side cheating, the Gurkhas were deployed to catch them out. This was particularly satisfying! Fortunately, we had a good team in the Headquarters who were well honed after Exercise Bold Guard, so we were able to deal with the host of visitors, media, fuel spillages, weather and other frictions of life pretty well.

As part of our preparations, I was required to visit and recce a training area called Stanford in Norfolk. Time was tight so I took a chance and asked if the RAF could get me there and bring me back a couple of hours later. The planners said they could but it would have to be in a Puma helicopter and it would be treated as a tactical training flight, so I would be flying there and back at speed at low level, hedge-hopping and avoiding power lines. If I could live with that, fine. I accepted and the crew arrived at the landing site to pick me up. I got in, strapped myself into the seat and was ready.

Tactical was right and I was glad I hadn't eaten lunch that day. The Puma tore across the ground, weaving over the hedges, following treelines and lifting to avoid power lines before sinking back to low level again. Somewhere near Oxford, I looked down to see fields and a barn. The cattle scattered as we shot over the barn and I saw splashed on the roof in bright white paint:

PISS OFF BIGGLES

"Did you see that?" I asked over the mike.
"Yep. He doesn't like us very much."
It was there on the way back as well. I felt sorry for the farmer but I had a great flight courtesy of a highly skilled crew.

Purple Warrior was a success and we came home to Tidworth happy with what we had done. This brought an end to my two-year stint in the brigade and I was instructed to go back to the Staff College on promotion to Lieutenant Colonel, this time as a member of the directing staff. It was another good posting. As I was leaving, David took me to a farewell lunch and informed me that I was to become a Member of the British Empire (MBE) in the New Year. A 'triple whammy': promotion, an award and a good posting. I had nothing to complain about and, as an added bonus, I could see more of Brendan at boarding school in Sherborne. Life had been kind to me in 1st Infantry Brigade and I left with some happy memories. The late Molly Rimmell, my ever loyal, competent and fiery PA, was a great ally throughout.

1987 brought another good family event. My Godfather's son, Graham Dawe, had been playing rugby for Launceston Rugby Club and was gaining a reputation as a class player at hooker. As well as his farming duties at Southcombe near Tavistock, he was building his fitness and skill levels in a barn converted into a gymnasium. He was immensely strong and would not give up or back down. Convinced that he needed to go further, his

Launceston supporter and friend referred him to the coach at Bath Rugby. Graham was invited up for a trial, played one game for the second team and became a regular choice for the first XV. At that time, Bath had a stellar team, studded with international players and Graham was called forward to the England training squad. He was selected to play against Wales and Ireland. As the international season ended, supporters were surprised to learn that he travelled twice a week from Tavistock to Bath to train and play. Real dedication. He went on to represent his club, country and Cornwall and we enjoyed going to see him play at Twickenham and the Rec Ground in Bath. We still meet at family occasions and matches whenever we can. Graham was not the only sportsman at the time. His brother Nick spent his early days as a professional jockey, racing over fences and travelling around the world to ride.

The same year, John Wilsey's wife Lizzie had been developing an idea with the Tidworth wives that was to catch on. They planned to hold an early Christmas Fair called Michaelmas Madness on behalf of the Army Benevolent Fund (later ABF: The Soldiers' Charity.) Tedworth House in Tidworth, Wiltshire, was the setting as it offered an historic building, easy access and parking. The girls worked hard to obtain the stall holders, promote the event, plan the layout and cook the lunch. It took much thought and coordination but, come the day, all was set. Late that night, Southern England was lashed by a huge storm as winds of up to 100mph tore through woods, towns and villages, causing huge damage to power lines, telephone connections and water supplies. Fallen trees cut off five of the six roads from our home in Winterslow to my offices in Tidworth. Jane and the team managed to get to Tedworth House and drive along the impressive tree-lined road, which was still clear, to the house to get everything ready. Despite the storm damage, true British grit ensured that the fair was well attended. A couple of hours later, four trees fell on to the driveway that could well have done serious harm to anyone leaving the fair. Thankfully, no damage was done. That was not the end of the Early Christmas Fair; the event was so successful that it has been repeated almost every year in the grounds of Tedworth House. I don't think the team expected the idea to catch on as it did but the ABF has done extremely well as a result.

My tour as a Brigade Chief of Staff was the ideal training base for me. It brought together my teaching from the Staff College and, while commanding a Gun Battery, I learned the benefits of good leadership, quality staff work and how to plan ahead, delegate work and set realistic deadlines. I was lucky to be supported by a keen and competent team who were determined to succeed. As Chief of Staff, I enjoyed the support of two outstanding Brigadiers, in John Wilsey and David Thomson, and never lacked direction. It was a good tour that would serve me well in the years to come.

STAFF COLLEGE AND THE BRIGHTON BOMB: PROTECTING THE MARGARETS

In 1984, the IRA exploded a massive bomb inside the Grand Hotel, Brighton. It was the time of the Conservative Party Conference and several high-profile politicians and their wives died and were injured in the blast. By sheer good fortune the Prime Minister, Margaret Thatcher, and her husband, Dennis, survived.

The IRA's response was chilling: "Today, you were lucky. But remember, we only have to be lucky once." Typical of the Prime Minister, she returned on the final day to give a rousing closing address and you could see it in her eyes: this lady would not be beaten.

Four years on, the hotel had been rebuilt and the Tories, still in power, were back for their next conference. Relieved of my teaching duties at the Staff College, I was tasked, as part of Operation RACOT, to go to Brighton and command the military element of the security plan in support of the Sussex Police Force.

I was briefed by the MOD and set off for Brighton to meet the police, three days before the conference was due to start. The Chief Constable was in overall command and the Assistant Chief Constable (Operations) acted as the officer in charge. Both were pleased to see me and took pains to ensure I was comfortable and had what I needed. The police's concern was that, having spent the last four years investigating the attack by the IRA, their teams could find no-one responsible or any intelligence that it was going to happen again. There was no greater priority than protecting Her Majesty's Government and its PM. And I had a special interest too that gave me added incentive; my godmother, Margaret Fry, had been staying in the Grand Hotel at the time of the bomb and thankfully survived. Now, she was back with her husband, John, as she was Chairman of the Conservative Conference. I had two Margarets to look after. I enjoyed ringing my Godmother's hotel room to tell her that I was in town and supporting her and that she would be OK. After all those times she and John had cared for me on holiday on the farm in Cornwall, I finally got the chance to repay them.

My military task force was sizable: I had a bomb disposal team fresh from Northern Ireland with its hi-tech equipment; a detachment of the anti-terrorist squad located in a secluded site to provide a rapid response in the event of a hostage situation or assault; and HMS Nurton, a minesweeper of the Royal Navy, patrolling Brighton sea front.

One evening, I went out with Peter Westcott, the police officer in charge of operations, to brief him on our plan. He was happy and I asked him if there was anything he was concerned about. He told me that he was worried about a barracks that was insecure. I thought that was odd because the MOD told me nothing about the place when I had asked the same question about vulnerable points. It was the only barracks that he was worried about because he thought it could well be a target for any terrorist who was looking for a soft touch.

I went to the barracks the following morning and demanded to see the base commander. He told me that he also thought his site was vulnerable, had reported it and got nowhere. It was a Territorial Army barracks and would be a totally unguarded location for the duration of the conference. He was frustrated and needed help.

Knowing that the police would be fully tied up during the conference and couldn't provide any support, I remembered that there was a Royal Green Jacket Battalion based in Dover. I called Ant Palmer, the Commanding Officer, and his reaction was spot on – he got the message immediately and said that he would have a guard force in place, armed and ready by the evening. True to his word, the soldiers appeared and the place was searched and secured for the duration of the conference. Assistant Chief Constable Westcott was delighted and it was an ideal response. Ant got us out of a hole with potential for real damage that day.

Thankfully, the conference went without a hitch. Working from our operations room, I had a good team and we enjoyed teaching a relatively inexperienced police force the skills and techniques of counter terrorism operations. We circulated a video showing a car containing 2lb of explosives (the weight of a bag of sugar) being exploded with devastating effects and that clearly demonstrated the importance of doing the job properly. I met the members of the mounted police patrol and, while we were often suspicious of the vehicles we found, we only disabled one suspect car. At the end of the conference, the Prime Minister came to our Police Headquarters to say thank you. I was able to tell her that one of my Bomb Disposal Team members had just been awarded a mention in dispatches for his last tour in the province but that he was too modest to tell her himself.

"Well done," said Mrs Thatcher.

"Bloody marvellous," said Dennis.

The PM then asked the operator if there was anything he needed to make his job any easier. Sensing his opportunity, he told her that there was a piece of kit that would make the robotic detector (called 'a wheelbarrow') more sensitive and manoeuvrable. He needed a couple of dozen, they were available and would cost a few thousand. Cheap and very effective. Turning to her secretary, the PM fixed him with a stare and said please get them.

I rang the MOD in the morning to warn them of the conversation. "Too late," I was told. "Number 10 rang first thing and told us to get the kit by lunchtime!" Impressive stuff and we knew we had to get it done. Mrs Thatcher would check.

I came home with the offer of a post-Service career in the police force from the Chief Constable ("Sorry, too busy to think about leaving the Army") and I submitted my post-tour report to the MOD. It had been a good job. Maybe we were lucky, too. We will never know but we certainly tried hard enough. And both Margarets were safe.

I had been given that Brighton job following a return to Staff College in 1987. It was a role that held little worry for me. I had been a student there some years before, was familiar with the routine of joining the directing staff and knew quite a few of the others going there on promotion as well. To begin with, Jane and I thought I could base myself at Camberley while she and our daughter Kate stayed in our house in Wiltshire. I moved in to the Mess and began my new role with the Staff Course. I became a member of one of the college's three divisions; mine was C division, under the watchful eye of the divisional colonel, a delightful Guards officer who had a natural way with people, put the students at their ease and used his sense of humour to excellent effect. He took a lot of interest in what I was doing and was a pleasure to work for.

The Commandant, Major General John Watters, was a senior officer I had met in Germany and I knew he was someone with very high standards. I had to get it right if I was to get through this. Fortunately, my early meeting with him came while I was leading an eighty-minute discussion on a complicated tactical concept. I had prepared well for it and he came in soon after I started, sat down and said little. Soon after sending the students out for the break (and for me, a cigarette) I came back into the room. He was still there and stayed until the end. *That's it*, I thought, *if he doesn't like it, my career could be over*. I heard nothing for quite a while, until the Deputy Commandant passed me in the corridor one day and said, "Oh, Freddie. The Commandant very much enjoyed your syndicate discussion the other day. Well done." Phew!

Usually, I could expect to spend one term as a teacher and then join one of the other teams involved in writing and preparing for the terms ahead. My own was the tactics team, something to which, again, I was well equipped to contribute, with my team leader Ian McGill – a very pragmatic, cheerful Royal Engineer with a South African background. But plans have a habit of changing and, for me, it meant that I had to teach for three full terms and only prepare the papers for the next term for one.

Teaching was a very busy time; preparing for and leading discussions with ten students; taking them on field exercises; setting and marking papers; and report writing. The weekends passed too quickly and I felt uneasy about living away from Jane and our home. So we decided to move up to Camberley, hired an agent to let the house and prepared to move.

It was by no means an easy decision, made worse by the appalling state of our allocated quarter; it was absolutely filthy.

I felt it was the duty of the Quartermaster, who was there at the time of the handover, to recognise the condition of the home with which I was being presented and do something about it. But he didn't and, with the removal lorry on its way to us and tenants moving in to our old place in Wiltshire, I felt I had no option and so I accepted the house. Big mistake. I should have refused it and, when Jane arrived and saw the condition of the quarter, she was understandably very upset, having spent the last weeks cleaning the house we had just left to an immaculate standard. I wrote to the previous occupant to complain about the position he had left us in. He did not accept this but, grudgingly, gave me a contribution towards the cost of the cleaning. I hoped that I would never have to serve with him or the Quartermaster again; it was a shockingly unprofessional way to behave. This taught me a valuable lesson about the importance of the quality of soldiers' housing that was to become a big issue during my time as Adjutant General much later on.

Life in Camberley soon improved. We enjoyed getting to know the students and other members of the directing staff who lived in the same road. Jane found a job locally and our daughter Kate was settling in to her first boarding school in Taunton; she would later join Brendan at King's College, across town. Being at home seemed very quiet when both of them were away but we enjoyed their holidays and short breaks as well. On the less busy days, we were lucky to be encouraged to join the golf club at Wentworth, a world-famous championship course in Surrey where it was common to see many of my golfing heroes playing the much-televised West Course. I played for the Staff College team and, often, Gil Bray would join us for weekends to play as well. This was a rare privilege and we made the most of it.

Time passed quickly and we entered 1988 in good shape. My teaching duties continued but with some added anticipation: I knew that, sometime in the year, I would be informed of the

Regiment I had been selected to command. There was only one I really wanted – my old Regiment, 3 RHA. The Regiment was then on an operational tour in Cyprus and I knew that they were not a happy bunch. The lads felt neither appreciated, valued nor, in short, 'loved'. A number of my old friends were ringing me up and asking, "We want you back; when are you coming?" Regiments like to know who the new CO is going to be; will he look after us and can he be trusted? I told them that I wanted to be appointed as their CO but I couldn't promise anything. Finally, the announcement came; I was selected to be CO 3 RHA, in mid-1989. The man who made that decision was Major General Peter Bonnet, then Director Royal Artillery and my Battery Commander from my very first tour with 40 Regiment. I rang him to thank him and he was very generous. But he did say that he was trusting me to do a good job and that it wasn't going to be easy. My phone calls to Cyprus reconfirmed this; I had to rebuild their confidence and restore their pride in themselves at what was going to be a busy time. But this was 3 RHA; we had done it before and we could do it again.

Restoring the pride and spirit of a Regiment depends crucially on two people – the CO and the Regimental Sergeant Major. The posting people rang me up; who did I want as my new RSM? "Who is the best?" I asked. McPherson. "Then that is who I want." Agreed.

I had never met Mr McPherson, known to all as Mac, but I knew him by reputation (which was impressive), so I thought it would be good to meet over lunch to get to know each other before we both moved back to Germany. Mac and his wife, Chris, arrived with their young children, Paul and Nicola, and their terrier. Minutes later, I looked out of the window to see the terrier fighting with our dog, Max, and the children riding across the grass having taken our children's bikes from the garage. Not the ideal start. We separated the dogs, rescued the bikes and enjoyed a good talk over lunch. We knew we would be too busy for pleasantries once we got to work. We got along very well indeed; Mac would be a wise counsellor and powerful ally on whom I could rely completely. Jane would also be good friends with Chris. I wrote my first directive and was feeling increasingly confident about my first few weeks in the Regiment.

My tour at the Staff College taught me some valuable lessons about the quality of officer candidates attending as students. I could quite easily recognise those who were idle and disinterested and others who were keen to learn and succeed. I knew that working with the latter would bring the greatest benefit and I watched their careers develop with interest. It was good to catch up with them as our paths crossed. My senior officers gave me good pointers for the future, particularly Brigadier Rupert Smith. I would see him again soon.

My Godmother
Margaret Louise Fry DBE

First rod and bad habit, aged 2
Southcombe, Milton Abbott
1953

My sister Carolyn Mason

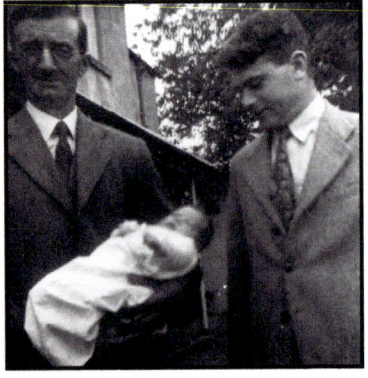

With my father Fred (right)
and Grandfather Dawe (left)
Southcombe, Milton
Abbott, Summer 1951

My Mother Ruth (left) with her older brother and my Godfather Reed and his wife Vera. Broadwoodwidger, Devon 2009

Helping farmhand Harvey, aged 3
Southcombe, Milton Abbott, summer 1954

Riding Sally to Gulworthy School,
aged 4, Gulworthy, Tavistock, Autumn 1956

First day at Wellington School, aged 11
Wellington, Somerset, Autumn 1962

With my fellow cadets. Richard Gregory Smith (in glasses) joined the Intelligence Corps and was killed in the Mull of Kintyre helicopter crash in 1994

Cadet trekking expedition led by David Elkington (centre); I'm on the second left. Peak District 1965

Sandhurst Crest

Winning the drill competition : Ypres Company winning the Drill
competition at Sandhurst. Colour Sergeant Terry Ewers is saluting
in the rear. I'm in the rear rank, second from the right
Royal Military Academy
Sandhurst, 1970

The Commissioning Parade:
I'm leading the Commissioning Parade on Old College Square
Royal Military Academy,
Sandhurst, April 1972

Major Peter Bonnet: My first Battery Commander. Our Leader, Northern Ireland, 1975

The Battery Intelligence Officer, just thinking: The Gasworks Northern Ireland, 1975

With Jane on our wedding day
Welshpool, Powys
July 14 1973

With my best man – and still my best friend – Gil Bray
Welshpool, Powys
July 14 1973

Rugby: J Battery Rugby Team in action. Launching Benny Benoit into the attack. Sgt 'Bugs' Bannister supporting behind me
Paderborn, Germany, 1978

MOD (1): Field Marshal Sir Edwin ('Dwin') Bramall's last day in the Army (in the striped tie). General Sir Tim Morony standing to his left (centre of steps)
MOD Whitehall, London, 1982

Staff College: Camberley, 1983

BATUS (1) Picnicking on the Canadian Prairie with Lieutenant Colonel Jonnie Hall (centre) and Capt Alastair Cuming
Batus, Canada
Summer 1985

BATUS (2) Tanks advancing across the Prairie, BATUS
Batus, Canada
Summer 1985

My cousin Graham Dawe; his first England
cap against Wales was in 1987
Twickenham Stadium

Protecting the Margarets: Margaret Thatcher at the
Conservative Party Conference, with my Godmother Margaret
Fry on her left (before the IRA bomb)
Brighton
1980

SERVE TO LEAD

BEST JOB (SO FAR)

We left Camberley for Paderborn to take command of 3 RHA, just returned from its operational tour in Cyprus. We knew that our stay would be brief as we were to return to Colchester in four months' time. The six month quarantine laws persuaded us to leave Max the dog with our friends, Tim and Annie Page, until our return. I don't think Max ever forgave us for doing that!

The Regiment was as I expected to find it. The men had clearly not had a happy tour and did not feel at all valued. Mac had just arrived as well and we spent the time walking around the barracks, talking to and getting to know the soldiers. We knew we would be busy and, taking training and other commitments into account, we had just a few weeks to prepare for the move to Colchester after eighteen years in Paderborn. The moving of units around the world (known as the 'Arms Plot') was a recognised and a normal activity at that time. The permanent bases in Germany, the UK and Cyprus all required units and Regiments to change locations from time to time, to ensure that those involved kept their skills and experience well-honed and refreshed. The same applied to those on short tour operational duties in places like Belize and Northern Ireland. But the instructions issued to the Regiment for the move were completely inadequate and we were at risk of getting things badly wrong. Mac saw it too and we knew that things had to change. I was very disappointed at how poor the planning had been. The author and man responsible had clearly been wasting his time for the six months he had been in Cyprus and he should have produced a plan that was far more effective. He had failed. Fortunately, he was due to move on soon and to this day doesn't know how lucky he was not to get sacked immediately. I looked elsewhere for help. Major Andrew Ritchie, by far my most effective Battery Commander, was moved up to become the Second in Command and I asked Major Paul Cook to take on the detailed planning for the move. Thankfully, they were perfect choices and it allowed me to concentrate on other things.

Knowing that the Regiment is run largely by its senior ranks – a key element that had been overlooked – I spent a lot of time talking to the sergeants in a quiet room with no officers present. I said that we had very little time to complete our tasks and wanted to know where our problems were. This was a once-only opportunity to get things off their chest. I had learned for myself the importance of listening – not talking – in leadership. So I said I would listen and change things where I could but, after that, I expected them, as my key players, to stop the whining and get on with it. Mac was with me throughout and heard it too. They spoke clearly about the need for support, career development and clear direction, and I hoped they felt better for doing so. Slowly, I began to detect the change: my boys were moving about with a smile and looking confident. I did the same thing with my officers and talked to them about what I expected from an RHA Officer – professional, confident but never arrogant (the latter was unfortunately all too present in some of our officers). Thankfully, I had good role models in Captain Roddy Campbell (calm, confident, with a real sense of humour) and Lieutenants James Learmont (highly professional), Joe Shone (a great character and a real 'two-steps forward and one step back' sort of guy; with Joe, parties went well but so did disasters), and Nic Parham (a very steady, reliable man). They had what I needed and expected. They did not disappoint.

Over the Christmas period 1989, some of my warrant officers took their wives to Berlin for a short break. The Berlin Wall fell at the time they were there and they gave me a commentary of these extraordinary effects from their hotel. The Cold War was at an end and no-one could predict the future. Within days, people from East Germany flooded over the border and drove into West Germany. My partner artillery Regiment from the German Army was tasked to establish emergency facilities on our local training area to provide tents, washrooms and catering for thousands who kept arriving, keen to make the most of what they could buy in the West, particularly Levi jeans, leather goods and music boxes. Satisfied and with a financial incentive from the German Government to go home, the crowds eventually left. The German Army had done well to look after some East Germans who were relieved to get away from the Warsaw Pact authorities. The potential humanitarian crisis had been averted.

The Berlin Wall drama began to settle down but, while we were still very busy with just a few weeks to go until we moved, I suddenly faced a major distraction, prompted by a pointless question from a fellow CO. He had the idea that, to make recognition of the Gunner soldiers based in Dortmund easier, he wanted to put diamond-shaped, plastic, coloured symbols behind the Artillery cap badge. Rather than just do it, he sent a request to the Royal Artillery Headquarters for the authority to proceed. But it provoked a row because, in an attempt to regularise our standards of uniform (an idea that came around rather too often), the Director Royal Artillery (DRA), our professional head, issued an edict: conform to the laid-down standard of dress. No exceptions. I appealed and said that I would comply in all respects but please let me keep the red backing to our Regimental cypher. For me, this defined what 3 RHA was and stood for.

The cypher commemorated the award of a Victoria Cross to one of our officers in the desert during WW2. The appeal was rejected and I was told to get on with it. I had a lot of difficulty with that and could see the effect this would have on my boys once I issued the order. Except for some wise counsel from Mac and two great Quartermasters with years of experience, I would have resigned and walked away from the Army. I had rarely felt that angry. The cypher represented the ethos and identity of the Regiment and it was being taken away without good reason. To a soldier, the Regimental insignia is vital to his/her core purpose, pride and sense of belonging. It frustrated me that I was not being heard and I felt that we were being bullied. It became a battle of wills and I was going to be the loser. I should perhaps have ignored it – my immediate superior operational commanders had little interest in what I was doing and even less in what the DRA was saying. But my lads did as asked and they never complained, though I could see that they could not understand it either and were angry, too.

Our move to Colchester was relatively trouble-free and we endured the usual frustrations when one Regiment is being replaced by another but time was too short to worry, when we were busy converting from one type of gun to another And I was very grateful to Major Bob Harmes, a good friend from my J Battery days in the mid-1970s, for the excellent work he did to keep things in good shape.

Our married quarter, a former Georgian farmhouse now behind the wire in Kirkee Barracks, was rumoured to be haunted and was just across the road from the Officers' Mess and Regimental offices; it was the same one that the CO lived in when 3 RHA was last stationed there in the 1970s. In fact, my Regimental Honorary Colonel General Dick Trant was the CO at that time and told me that he wrote the orders for deploying his men to Northern Ireland for its first tour from the same study that I was using. Dick also talked about arranging a drinks party to meet important and helpful military and civilians in the local community and introduce his newly arrived Regiment to them. I was in much the same situation as Dick and decided to do the same. Invitations were sent out, the Gunner band was booked and I instructed that the officers, wives and partners should see this as a three line whip for hosting. It was a 'must attend'.

Going home one evening, I found Jane in a pretty frosty mood. Asking her if we had a problem, she said: "Yes. Why are you being so difficult to Joe Shone?"

Surprised and, after a little probing, I discovered that Joe had been to see Jane for tea that afternoon. She saw that he had something on his mind and he told her his problem. Joe, a very accomplished horseman from his days in Zimbabwe, explained that he had entered a pairs' jumping competition at the Windsor Horse Trials. He had found a partner and two mounts from the King's Troop but he could not go now because the CO had ordered the three line whip for the party that evening. He said he stood a good chance of winning and really wanted to take part. Jane took pity.

"I've said he should go," she said. Doubting that he could win, I agreed reluctantly and said he had better get back in time to host at the party. Joe did get back, this time clutching the trophy and dressed for the jumping competition. I'm glad he didn't say, "Told you so," even if he thought it. Joe had style, I will give him that. He later went on to win the gold medal in the

Welsh Cambrian Patrol competition, which was a marvellous test of military skills.

Part of our move to Colchester involved taking over from the last Regiment and converting to a new gun, the 155mm FH 70. This was not an easy conversion as the gun is a complicated system and the crew does not benefit from the cover offered by the Abbot. It is also towed behind a large tractor and sometimes requires a police escort on long road moves. To accustom the crews to living and operating outdoors, our first exercise was to the Otterburn training area, close to my recruiting area in Newcastle. Our move made the headlines as one of our guns broke down on the well-known bridge over the Tyne. It was not planned but the TV coverage did no harm in attracting young soldiers to join us.

Otterburn is a demanding training area and an ideal way to introduce soldiers to the demands of living rough. The weather is often harsh, the mosquitoes and midges in the Kielder forest very aggressive, and the gun and vehicle often get stuck on the narrow routes. It is excellent value. We were there at the time of the World Cup and I knew my football-mad soldiers were desperate to see England play. I asked Mac to hire some rooms, a bar, transport and enough TVs for the Regiment but told him to say nothing to the soldiers. He secured the NAAFI and instructed another visiting cadet force to find a better place, or risk the wrath of a Regiment of wet, dirty and tired Geordie soldiers who want to see the football. The cadet commander withdrew.

As the day approached, all was ready and I could see that the soldiers were getting more and more worried: would the CO let us see the game? Bob Harmes picked up on this and said that my blokes would not remember the day's firing programme but would never forget that I didn't let them see the football. He was dead right, of course, but I said nothing. As the time went on, the men were getting more and more anxious. Eventually, with just enough time to spare, I ordered, "Cease firing. Return to camp." Morale soared. The only disappointing bit was that England drew their match, so we had to do it all over again later on. England won and my men remembered seeing two games, if nothing else. I enjoyed the wind up.

Colchester was a fun place and the long weekends allowed my boys to go home to Newcastle or wherever and get back again in good time. Jane and I seemed to spend all our time driving to collect the children to and from boarding school in Taunton, a trip of about five hours. Back home, we soldiered on in our new barracks and found our neighbour units to be a good and helpful bunch. Collectively, however, we COs found our new Brigade Commander to be a difficult man to read and I for one never thought he really trusted me. Happily, we were left alone to get on with it and I was given terrific support from our Honorary Colonel whenever I asked. Sadly no longer with us, Dick Trant was a warm-hearted, generous man. He was survived by his lovely wife, Tinks. We miss them both.

The invasion of Kuwait by Iraq in the 1990s brought a sharp focus to our lives. Saddam Hussein resisted all demands by the UN to withdraw and a strong US-led coalition was assembled. Our part in this was to provide the necessary reinforcements of trained manpower from the UK. We took great care in selecting our soldiers because we were determined not to let down the 1st armoured division in the US army structure, led by General Rupert Smith (for whom I had huge respect). So we said farewell to the team and they set off for 1st division based in Germany. We spent a long time looking after the families left behind – news was hard to come by – and we watched developments with growing concern. Eventually, Saddam refused to budge and the invasion to kick him out was launched. It succeeded with big losses on the Iraqi side but mercifully few on our own. We welcomed them home with a sigh of relief; they had all made it and came back with great stories to tell.

As summer arrived, we began to plan for our summer ball. It was a fairly traditional format and I thought that the event itself went well enough, although I detected that some of my younger officers were muttering about it a few days later and clearly weren't very happy. Inquiring further, they said it was boring, not very imaginative and didn't have enough lady socialites from London present. I said that, if they could do better, they were welcome to try. One named David Harrington accepted the challenge, we agreed the date and the theme. It was to be a James Bond night. Unbeknown to me, David's gang contacted Pinewood Studios and requested if they could borrow as many Bond film props and memorabilia as possible for a high grade party. Amazingly, Pinewood agreed and said that, if transport and insurance could be arranged, the studio would open its doors. The kit started to arrive and included Goldfinger's Aston Martin DB5 (battered but still in working order), SMERSH and SPECTRE flags, fake crocodiles, casino tables and collapsing sofas among many other examples. The Officers' Mess building provided a perfect backdrop and setting for the party. I attended in a DJ and was amazed to see so many scantily dressed young ladies everywhere. I discovered that a towel can conceal a great deal. Sean Connery was the only thing lacking and I had to admit that David's party was much better than the one I had arranged and I enjoyed telling him so. I also enjoyed taking the Aston out around the barracks.

The year progressed and we struggled to meet the increasing demands of operational commitments at a time of under-manning and it was a juggle, mixed with some risk, to achieve the troop levels required in Belize, Northern Ireland and the Falkland Islands and to conduct exercises in Cyprus and Kenya. Absent soldiers means a lot of single parents and our Quartermaster, Bob Harmes, devoted almost all of his time to looking after them. Bob did a fabulous job and Jane, Mac's wife Chris and Bob's wife Pauline spent many days out with the families on their various activities. Sadly, we were to attend Pauline's funeral some years later. She was an ideal role model to Jane as a young wife in J Battery and showed her what it meant to belong to a caring family.

Sadly, we dealt with a young soldier who lost his life in Belize through a tragic accident. I happened to be visiting the soldier's Battery with Richie Drewett, Mac's successor as RSM at the time. The Battery was in a remote area and I went to the Headquarters to arrange a flight and find out the details. The soldier was a corporal called Holt and all we knew was that he had shot himself in the head. The Headquarters staff there were very nervous about the news leaking out and tried to prevent me from contacting anyone. I ordered them to connect me with the Regiment at home immediately. I got through to the man's Officer Commanding, told him to get hold of Jane as soon as possible and go round to see his wife to tell her what we knew. It was the right thing to do because, within minutes of Jane's arrival, the wife of another soldier in Belize turned up at her door to tell the widow what she had heard. It was a good example of how the rumour mill can go badly wrong before the facts are known. I was glad I insisted on making the call and I hoped the difficult staff officer was embarrassed at being so defensive.

Otherwise, my team all came home safely. By then, at the end of my time as a CO, I knew that I was to move on, this time on promotion and a return to the MOD. My successor was to be Lieutenant Colonel David Richards, a contemporary from the days when we were together in 3 RHA. David was a friend and I knew that my boys would be well looked after and would trust him. His wife, Caroline, would be just right for our families, too. We handed over on our way home after the Regiment's annual reunion dinner and, as we neared Colchester, he said, "Don't worry, Freddie. I will look after them." I knew he would and was happy to leave them in good hands and with great memories of some top-flight people. Two and a bit years later, I heard that David Richards, in almost his last act before handing over command again, told 3 RHA to replace the red backing behind the cypher. He had righted a wrong – at last! We have been wearing it ever since.

David went on to have a spectacular career, described well in his autobiography *Taking Command*, and he became a peer after his time as Chief of the Defence Staff. Knowing that we had a friend like David as CDS, as well as many other senior officers who had commanded 3 RHA in the intervening years, was very re-assuring for the future of our Regiment and the people in it. Soldiers need to have a purpose if recruiting and retention is to work successfully.

We moved to a new quarter in London and I began to adjust to a common trait called 'Post Command Blues' – doing a great job then suddenly giving it up leads to an adjustment shock. Being a CO means that for nearly three years, whatever you do, you do it for your Regiment. Then it all stops and you give up the quarter, the car and the team around you. You go from being the main man to just another faceless person in a suit in the MOD, not being in charge any longer, like a managing director who has lost his company. It can make you question your relevance and takes a while to get used to.

Fortunately, the pace of life in the MOD helped me overcome that. But CO was without doubt the best job I'd had, or was ever likely to have… or so I thought at the time.

BACK TO THE MOD

I was promoted to the rank of Colonel in 1992 and sent to work in the Directorate of Defence Policy where, following a reorganisation a few months after I arrived, my new boss was to be Ms Margaret Aldred. A highly intelligent, efficient and experienced lady, she was impressive and became a good mentor to me. Her workload was prodigious.

The Directorate was a busy place and I soon realised that my knowledge of the detail of British Defence Policy was pretty thin. I'd had just over two and a bit years enjoying command of 3 RHA and not paying much attention to what was going on around me but it was a dangerous time. Internationally, the UK was facing a complex and fast changing environment; the Cold War was at an end, the countries of the former Warsaw Pact had fractured and looked to join NATO for its Defence and Security needs. Russia was suspicious, uncertain of its role in the world and struggling to draw down its troop levels and capability. Its navy and air force were crumbling. Further afield, the rigid control exercised by the USSR during the Cold War had gone and tensions were already apparent in the nations of the Balkans, the near and Far East.

At home, the Treasury had changed the financial accounting rules, giving budget holders the resources, responsibility and accountability for delivery. There was blithe and naïve talk in Government of a 'Peace Dividend' and reductions in numbers of people and capability in defence across the Navy, Army and Air Force were being addressed. Lessons from the first Gulf War were emerging and did not make for comfortable reading. There was growing pressure on the defence budget from the Treasury to make big 'efficiencies' – polite language for 'cuts'.

Dialogue with our allies was important, so we continued our programme of Defence Staff Talks with our NATO partners and with the former Warsaw Pact countries, most of whom were looking for ideas on how best to structure their approach, learn about the workings of the UK Government and the MOD in particular and deal with their own specific problems. We travelled every two months or so to France, Germany, Greece and Poland and a host of other countries.

I remember the visit to the Pentagon in Washington DC well. The UK and US teams gathered in the vast, bewildering Pentagon building and presented their respective defence and security policies. We enjoyed an open and frank discussion that showed how much we had in common as both Governments bore down on defence structures to achieve benefit from the fall of the Berlin Wall. During the talk, the door opened and in came General Colin Powell, Chairman of the US Joint Chiefs of Staff and the most senior officer in the Pentagon. He was best known for his role during the liberation of Kuwait where he established a worldwide reputation as a statesman. We brought him up to date with our discussion and, for about thirty minutes he demonstrated his complete mastery of the strategic, economic and political world of the 1990s. Relaxed, confident and assured, he came across as an inspirational commander and a man whom I would always respect and follow. Rising to leave, he promised that he would take every opportunity to challenge the UK Government on their least attractive military options and fight for the continued relevance of NATO. We were pleased to hear it.

Our time in Washington was not all work and no play. We were entertained by our American colleagues at a delightful restaurant in Georgetown. Founded in 1751, Georgetown is one of the oldest and most historic parts of Washington. With Paul Flaherty, an excellent man from the MOD, we visited the Kennedy Space centre, the White House and the Abe Lincoln Memorial. Given a day off from our talks, Paul and I travelled past the CIA headquarters at Langley into Pennsylvania's familiar Amish country to tour the Battle of Gettysburg. The museum brought the battle of July 1863 to life and explained the tactics and the fish hook advantages of General Meade's Union Troops and the impact on the Confederates of having to fight on external lines, led by General Robert E Lee. The presentation over, we then met our guide, a retired official from the State Department. Hearing that we were from the MOD in London, that I was a Gunner and Paul a civil servant, he offered us the full tour and, for the next three hours, took us around the sites and explained the actions at Cemetery Ridge, Little Round Top, the Wheatfield and Colonel Pickett's Bayonet Charge. He showed why Gettysburg became known as the High Water Mark of the Civil War and how both sides suffered such heavy casualties (46-51,000 soldiers). In November of that year, Lincoln visited the battlefield and gave the brilliant Gettysburg address. A total of 272 words that took two minutes to deliver. Pure magic. Gettysburg is a must-see for any visit to the States and I would recommend a viewing of the film *Gettysburg* before the trip.

Our trip to Kiev in the Ukraine gave us another Eastern European perspective. The end of the Cold War was still fresh in the memory and senior leaders were struggling to find direction and ideas. Ukraine is a fiercely independent country where initiative was not welcomed. The Russians called it Ukraine, meaning 'on the edge' and they were right, in geography and attitude. We had to be careful to be seen as helpful without appearing arrogant or condescending. As our talks went on, our hosts were offhand initially but soon became more relaxed and friendly. On the first evening with our hosts, we were taken to a hotel with low lighting, burly, shaven-headed men in dark glasses, expensive cars outside and beautiful women at the bar. *Someone is doing well out of this situation*, I thought.

The second night was a trip to the opera, performed live in a grand setting before an audience with lots of empty seats. My host told me that this event occurred every night, regardless of the attendance. I said that I was surprised that the opera could continue and survive in that way. "It has to," he said. "Opera is part of our culture and we will not lose it." It told me a lot about the Ukrainian spirit. But returning to the airport in convoy for the flight home, our Ukrainian conscript turned and gave me a surprised, confused look as he held up the gearstick in his hand. I said nothing as his black Zil staff car came to a halt and we swapped cars and baggage. *Still some way to go*, I thought.

The best visit, by far, was to Japan. Following WW2, Japan was constrained from talking to other countries, so this trip was at their invitation. We accepted with pleasure and, given that none of us had been there before, we asked for guidance from the Foreign Office on how best to behave in their country. We were advised that it was rude to be late, that 'Yes' might mean 'No' and that golf and karaoke were national passions – the Japanese went to night school to practice performing their songs and golf ranges were everywhere in Tokyo.

The city is huge; on one occasion we travelled by helicopter to a distant town and it took twenty minutes of flying before we even left the city of Tokyo. The Japanese were keen for us to experience their culture. Raw fish, rather like their music, is definitely an acquired taste and an evening of karaoke in a night club where I was asked (ordered) to get on stage and sing *House of the Rising Sun* went well enough. The audience applauded politely but I took some teasing.

As the year went on, I began to understand the nature of the Civil Service that controls the bureaucracy in the MOD and realise that we are different beasts. The civil servant, often referred to as 'the Colleague', has a primary role and that is to ensure that what goes on in the Ministry and is done on behalf of Defence is necessary and appropriate. Ideas that are seen to be novel and contentious are rarely followed through. The media's increasingly intrusive role, where the actions of government are probed with scepticism and are often heavily criticised, has a limiting effect. The Government of the day has become a convenient target and this leads to a wish by civil servants to protect their Minister. It makes them highly risk averse. The military, on the other hand, are trained to embrace and be comfortable with risk and this culture clash can lead to a good deal of frustration and argument. It isn't helped by the fact that everyone inside the MOD, unless on duty elsewhere, goes to work in a suit and so the two tribes are indistinguishable one from the other. I was always a strong advocate of letting us work in uniform, as already happened in several NATO countries, as it would differentiate us and let everyone know which culture we were coming from as we met to iron out the issue of the moment. Probably too novel and contentious an idea to make the grade. And the terrorist threat precluded us from doing it. That threat was reinforced when the IRA fired a mortar bomb from a truck parked by the road just outside the MOD into the gardens of No 10 Downing Street.

My second year saw a much improved approach. Bruce

Mann, a highly competent operator and experienced civil servant, began to quantify precisely what was required of Britain's Defence Forces in what was described as the Defence Programme Directory. This was very serious, grown-up stuff – the Chancellor's defence budget depended on it – and we had to get it right. Many hours were spent in discussion and the finished product was, for the first time, something that we could use when arguing for resources.

But the pressure to find savings did not relent and a new initiative was launched. This time, the Government introduced something called the Defence Costs Study, a review of all Defence's activities from the MOD downwards, to improve processes and identify savings across the Board. Margaret Aldred was to join the team coordinating this work with Richard Hatfield as her co-leader. I asked if I could work for her and, happily for me, she accepted.

This was really hard work; long hours set against a demanding schedule, with all three Services protecting their vested interests and resisting change that, in their view, went against their desire to protect what they had. It taught me a lot about the workings of the MOD, the motives of the Army, Navy and Air Force and, again, the effect that a determined minister can have on achieving the desired outcome: "find the savings, quickly." Actually, the report produced was a good piece of work and, eventually, it did lead to a better way of working. Only the Service's Medical Organisation felt badly treated and quoted the study often in their criticism. Admiral Sir Jonathon Band, later to become Head of the Navy, was a great help to me in this exercise.

In the course of my final year, I learned that I was to be promoted and sent to command the Artillery Group in the 3rd Division, based in Wiltshire. This was good news on three fronts: first, I got promoted; secondly, my boss was to be Major

General Mike Jackson, know to us all as 'Jacko', a man I liked and admired hugely; and thirdly, we were to live much closer to our children, boarding in the South West. And the dog would get a good walk around Salisbury Plain.

Prior to my posting, I had to complete the third and most enjoyable stage of my time at the Staff College.

Some twenty officers identified as having the ability to succeed embarked on a three-month Higher Command and Staff course to study the planning and conduct of military operations at the highest strategic level. Lectures with some of our most able military historians, including the late Dr Brian Holden Reid, the late Dr Richard Holmes and Keith Simpson, who was later to become an MP, were supported by discussions and table-top exercises to bring the lessons to life. Small pieces of written work were required to encourage research and I found a 5,000-word dissertation about the conduct of multinational operations surprisingly easy (despite managing to delete the work when it was almost finished and having to start again. Fortunately, I made the deadline and learned the importance of backing up my work). My next posting to the Balkans was to validate much of my research.

The highlight of the course for me was a tour of the battlefields of Europe in WW2 where I was led by an old mate from our days in Tidworth called Aldwyn Wight, a tough Welsh Guardsman and Falklands veteran who had the constitution of an ox; if the course had gone on for much longer, I think I would have been sent home for my own good. Aldwyn drove the car we had been allocated (far too fast for European roads) and once got lost en-route to the Belgian border, which upset the French officer who was travelling with us. He feared for his life. Aldwyn was persuaded to turn round just in time.

Soon after our return, it was time to bring the course to a close. It was high-grade and had set me up well for what was to follow. The world was becoming a dangerous place and the British Army was to play a central role in it. My next experience became another real adventure as the civil war in the Balkans raged.

BOSNIA
(FIRST TIME)

I joined the Headquarters and Artillery Group at 3rd Division, which was commanded by Jacko, in the spring of 1994. The end of the Cold War had drawn back the Iron Curtain and age-old tensions were exposed, particularly in the Balkans where years of civil war raged between the Serbs, Bosnians and Muslims in Bosnia Herzegovina. Territorial disputes were fuelled by the death of Tito, a Croat who had ruled Yugoslavia and kept ethnic ambitions in check with a rod of iron. The carving of his clenched fist dominated the hills above the town of Prozor in Croatia as a reminder. In Bosnia, the Serb leader and politician Milosevic led a force commanded by Ratko Mladic under the political authority of Radovan Karadic and opposed by a loose federation of Bosnian and Muslim forces. The fighting swept across the country, minefields were laid through and around contested front lines and the population began to flee abroad. The 'ethnic cleansing' of Bosnian and Muslim people was underway.

Many civilians – men, women and children – were held in concentration camps; homes and businesses were looted and burned; thousands were killed. It was a grim time in Europe and the media featured the brutality regularly; commentators such as Martin Bell and Kate Adie pushed the UK for more military involvement to stop the killing. We monitored the action regularly at our divisional operations briefings and began to see that this might be a fight in which 3rd Division could be involved. Our training reflected this change in mission: the Cold War was over, our business now was about peace support operations and, maybe, peacekeeping.

Interspersed to keep the two sides apart was the United Nations Protection Force (UNPROFOR), based in Sarajevo under the command of General Mike Rose, a soldier with immense operational experience. His book *Fighting for Peace* is a highly recommended read. His bodyguard was known as Goose. (A good ally of Jim Davidson and a great soldier, I was to see more of him in later life when I got involved in Jim's charity Care After Combat). A multinational force was deployed around the country but, typically, there were not enough troops to cover all the vulnerable areas of conflict. This was not helped by the UN's rules of engagement – soldiers in blue berets were not permitted to get involved in the conflict and employ force. This was a self-defence role and the opposing forces knew it. Knowing where the UN troops were based allowed the fighting to flow around and fill the empty spaces; factions were free to carry out their brutal activity unchecked.

The crisis in Srebrenica was a tipping point; led by Mladic, Serb forces entered the town and, unopposed by the resident Dutch force, proceeded to corral the Muslim population. Thousands of men, women and children were marched into the buildings, woods and forests and slaughtered. Their bodies were left where they were killed, with whatever they were carrying scattered around. It was a grim scene and a blatant war crime. Once the media heard, they flocked to the scene and an international story exploded as images were flashed around the world. Martin Bell's plea for NATO engagement grew even louder. In the Headquarters of the United Nations in New York, and at home in the MOD in London, there was a real feel of 'something must be done'. This civil war had to stop now, and there were signs that the factions were war weary and looking for a solution. The opportunity was there. Meanwhile, the killing continued.

The military constraints imposed by the UN led to an essentially static force without teeth, unable to act or intervene quickly, so the MOD and Foreign Office came up with the answer: we needed a UN Rapid Reaction Force (RRF) to go where ordered, quickly, and get engaged. The problem: we lacked a Concept of Operations (in effect, a plan for how the UN would carry out its tasks against various scenarios), signed up to and agreed by the UN contributing nations. Jacko called me in.

"Freddie, is there any reason why you can't re-arrange what you are doing for the next month or two?"

This was the summer of 1995 and our programme was pretty flexible; sensing that this had something to do with Bosnia, I replied, "Not really."

"Good; I want you to take a small team to Zagreb and write the Concept of Ops for the RRF, please."

"How long have I got?"

"You leave next week and I need it done soonest, so just a few weeks. Keep your ears and eyes to the ground. We might be joining you out there later."

Over the next two or three days, my team assembled, I said goodbye to Jane and we flew to Zagreb, the capital of Croatia and the genesis of the civil war between Bosnian and the Serbian Armies. Our hotel was full of Croatian refugees expelled by the Serb force. They were a distressing sight.

The headquarters in Zabreb was my first port of call and I

met the senior commanders led by General Bernard Janvier, an experienced officer and commander from the French Foreign Legion who spoke only a little English. My French was by then very rusty but it improved quite quickly (I was again very grateful to David Elkington for all that time he gave me at school).

My first visits to Bosnia soon showed just how difficult this job was going to be; there were competing agendas in the UN everywhere. By no means did all the international players agree that we were doing the right thing, believing they – and only they – had the right answer. We soon realised that our activities were being reported back to nations' capitals and that this was going to be a hard task. I began to think I should contact Jacko and ask to be pulled out. But, by then, Brigadier Robin Brims, a highly competent man (the best of my generation in my view, actually) and an old friend from our first time at the Staff College, had deployed with his Airmobile Brigade to the dock at Ploce Harbour in Croatia to act as the RRF. So, the die was cast and I decided that I would knuckle down, write the concept and get back to UK quickly. Jacko's 3rd Division was in the frame to implement the end of hostilities and I did not want to miss this deployment.

We watched General Janvier struggle to deal with the Serbs' siege of enclaves like the town of Gorazde – despite the gallant efforts of the affected Battalion's Commanding Officer John Riley – and the other UN safe areas, while the UN continued to refuse us the authority to act; and we watched General Rupert Smith (who had replaced Mike Rose in Sarajevo) as he fought to achieve a workable solution – again without the muscle – and Robin, who still did not have the authority to deploy over the border. After much frustration, we produced the Concept of Operations. It was by no means a perfect document and, with time, we could have improved it, but it would have worked and my team did a sterling job to get us there. So, another lesson: Good Enough is the enemy of the Best.

Janvier received the Concept, was very grateful and agreed that I could take my people home once the RRF Implementation Team, under the British General Pennefether, had arrived. I'm not sure what happened to the Concept after I handed it in and can only assume that it was never tested. I doubt that the frictions I saw in the Headquarters in Zagreb would ever allow it. We left about a day later. I was glad to go after two months but it did give me a good grounding and understanding of the Bosnian war, its players and personalities. It would pay dividends later.

Later that year, it was clear that the warring factions had had enough of the fight and wanted to stop. The UN gathered all the major parties together in Dayton, Ohio to thrash out the peace deal and, after much haggling over borders and things like weapon concentration areas, timings and the prisoner exchange programme, the Dayton Agreement was eventually signed with much fanfare. The UK contribution within NATO's force structure was to be 3rd Division, as we expected (despite a last minute bid for it to be changed to the 1st Division based in Germany. This was a very cheeky attempt to steal the glory, which was rejected by John Wilsey, now the Commander in Chief and my old brigade commander, who rang me to ask what I thought of the proposal. I told him!).

We launched into a frantic period of preparation of vehicles, recces, work up exercises, kit for the shipping and departure programmes. Winter was closing in and we had a very tight deadline to meet if Dayton was to work and the factions were to hold to their commitments.

In December, the shipping and equipment began to leave Marchwood Port and my team and I flew to Split Airport in Croatia. Replacing Brigadier Richard Dannatt's headquarters, our base was to be in an old place called the 'Tom' Factory in Gornji Vakuf, a town in central Bosnia. I like to think that the allocation of the division's area of responsibility, with the

Americans to the east and French to the south, was a happy one because of the renowned book *Eastern Approaches*. It tells the story of Fitzroy Maclean, an agent of Winston Churchill's Special Operations Executive, who in the 1940s was parachuted into Croatia to meet up with Tito's partisans and support them in their resistance to the Germans. He landed in the small town called Mrkonjic Grad (which this time was now manned by our Engineer Regiment), and his story goes on to reference many of the sites that were to become familiar to us in the months ahead. *Eastern Approaches* is a fine book and Maclean was a brave man.

Our accommodation was basic. It was the winter and very, very cold, with snow on the surrounding hills and valleys. Gornji Vakuf was the scene of some heavy fighting; there were minefields all over the place. The driving conditions were dangerous, with icy roads falling into steep gullies above fast flowing rivers. Going out every day was extremely high risk but we were under pressure to find habitable places to locate our soldiers and their equipment.

Travelling around the country by Land Rover or helicopter was a sobering experience. The evidence of ethnic cleansing was plain to see as the population fled from the towns, villages and farms to safer areas. The houses and buildings were empty and the warring factions had painted their own Regimental and unit insignia on the walls to show that they had been through the area. Unless the buildings had been set alight, the roofs were generally intact but the windows and doors had been removed and taken away, ready for the evacuees to find a place and start again. There was no power and, as we drove through the dark and freezing night, we came across ghostly images of wild animals roaming through unlit streets in search of food. Breaking down in the countryside, miles from anywhere, was a bad move and we took care to tell the Headquarters where we were going and our expected arrival and return time. Some of the local people did try to struggle on and it was not uncommon to see farmers moving on horse-drawn carts, loaded with hay, returning to their run down farms. The hayrick was built around a single long pole that stuck out from the back of the cart, not unlike a spear. It was almost impossible to see these carts in the blizzard with no lights, so driving into one of these poles could have been lethal for me or my driver. It took both of us to keep our eyes on the road if we were to stop in time. Tiring but essential.

Soon it became clear to us that this was not just a struggle of the late 20th Century. As I drove and flew around Bosnia, I saw many towns and villages in the same condition. Many were overgrown and I could see the evidence of the German occupation forces in WW2. It was not difficult to imagine the brutality that had occurred in that time.

We knew we had to ignore what we were seeing and get on. Dayton allowed us to do this but we had to be careful: we were not an army of occupation but a stabilisation force. Fortunately, most of the local people knew who we were and we were tolerated, if reluctantly. Language was a problem, so learning the basics of Serbo-Croat helped to break the ice. The minefield threat was real and we lost an officer and soldier of the division's cavalry reconnaissance Regiment, the Royal Lancers. Two more of my officers survived mine strikes over the next few days and were only saved by their Warrior armoured vehicles. It was a worrying time and we took some common sense precautions that allowed us to do our job as quickly and safely as we could.

I deployed with six heavy, long-range guns, supported by six more light ones already there, to give us the flexibility to occupy positions quickly and cover the areas as required. The heavy guns took time to arrive, so we were able to find bases and get them ready: logging factories, industrial sites, abattoirs and farm buildings all found a use and required top-to-bottom cleaning.

On Christmas day, I managed to get a lift aboard the Royal Navy Sea King helicopter on a flying visit up to Mount Igman, overlooking Sarajevo. Here Richard Lungmuss, the Battery Commander, had deployed his six light guns, ready to support the firing plan should it be ordered by General Rupert Smith. His soldiers had taken over from and were living in pre-prepared defensive positions that must have looked very like the trenches of WW1. His gun positions had the cover to store the ammunition and operate in the freezing conditions, if necessary for days. His men were all wearing red and white Father Christmas hats and were making the best of the day. Morale was high and I shared out the few goodies that we took up on our flight. Moving over to Richard's resident French Foreign Legion unit that was giving him some protection, I was able to thank Brigadier Subaru for his help. He was undoubtedly a very tough guy who spoke little English and I hope my French came up to scratch. Subaru was a good soldier and the men he was leading were equally so. More than a match for anything the Serbs had.

The ongoing heavy guns deployment into Split harbour was successful and my ever loyal and reliable driver, Bombardier Callaghan, and I spent hours driving around the country, checking out routes and other obstacles. It was a dangerous business as the conditions threatened to throw us off the cliffs into the river below and we were often out all night getting to the different places. Callaghan was a good man to have around and we became good friends and experts at fitting and removing snow chains in record time.

On our arrival, and back in Gornji Vakuf, Martin Bell was delighted to see us and asked if he could help. I wanted the factions to know that NATO had arrived and that the rules had changed; Dayton applies now and we were not to be messed with. I asked Martin to film my blokes deploying their light guns, talk to the soldiers and produce a good piece for TV. He did everything I wanted and the BBC devoted most of the news programme to us. I thanked him and promised that he could have what he wanted (more filming material for his documentary, for example) but, sadly, he said he was being called back. While local TV was staying, the story had already moved on and Martin was needed elsewhere. Kate Adie left soon afterwards.

As our deployment was underway, we discovered a potential glaring deficiency. In the rush to load the equipment at Marchwood and sail to Split docks in Croatia, we found that our Met troop had come away without any helium facility. The troop was responsible for calculating the weather conditions by launching a balloon and identifying wind speed and direction, air temperature, pressure and density at different altitudes. Without helium I had no ability to launch the balloon and my only recourse to remain accurate was to fire a round, observe and calculate the effect on the ground. Given the terrain, conditions and situation in Bosnia, that was not an acceptable alternative. I contacted my higher headquarters in UK for advice, only to be told that the staff and unit had broken up for Christmas leave and my opposite number had gone skiing. Frustrated and thinking hard for a solution, I suddenly remembered that Jonathon Band, my naval colleague from our MOD days, was now captain of HMS Illustrious. She was afloat somewhere in the Adriatic, supporting the NATO maritime effort, and could make helium for me. I rang Jonathon and, over a crackly telephone link, explained my difficulty. He saw the point straight away, agreed to provide what we needed and the helium containers arrived by Sea King helicopter on the next day. It was a great response and an example of real inter-Service cooperation. I was very grateful to Jonathon for his help. A little later, and with Illustrious safely back in Portsmouth, we attended a number of fun social events with Jonathon and Sarah Band aboard. It was a pity that Lusty was eventually sent off to the scrapyard. She was a much-loved vessel.

The town at one site called Sanski Most, was covered in hundreds of dead pigs, slaughtered by the Serbs as they left to return to their own territory. The carcases were everywhere but, because it was so cold, they were frozen and so did not present a health hazard. But we knew that we had to remove them before spring and only had a few weeks to do it. Funeral pyres appeared everywhere as the pigs were piled high and burned. It was not a pretty sight or smell. Roast pork lost its appeal for a while.

Having cleared the pigs from the wood factory in Sanski Most, we selected the site as a base for one of our gun batteries. There was plenty of material and space to build the soldiers' accommodation and secure the guns and ammunition. Some weeks later, Bosnia was visited by entertainers from the Combined Services Entertainment, or CSE show. Sanski Most was selected as our site and we used the material to build the stage, lighting and sound for the show. Fish was the headline act and, with his band (Marillion), was best known for his hit song *Carrie*. We assembled the soldiers for the show, Fish appeared in his vest and kilt, sounding not unlike Billy Connolly, and began his list of rock songs. Soon into his programme, the sky was lit up by tracer fire over the camp, rather like a firework display, coming from the town across the river. Fish looked up and said, "What's that?" Tracer, we replied. "F***k it," he said, "Turn it up." The volume was increased to match the amount of tracer flying over our base. The blokes loved Fish and he gave us a great show, dishing out as much banter as he got from the crowd. A true rock star.

As Christmas approached, Dayton gave us a demanding timetable to achieve the faction's troop withdrawals, weapon and equipment holding areas and minefield clearance. Part of the Dayton Agreement directed the factions to conduct prisoner handovers at selected points and times. A roadside hotel in our area, called Black Dog, was the place selected to conduct the handover. We deployed to meet and monitor the faction handover party and, at the appointed time in the ice and snow, the vehicles arrived. The lorries were empty but, as we approached, the smell coming from the canopy had me retching. It was the smell of death and the floor of the truck was covered. The faction was getting rid of its legacy of corpses and they were piled up for us to dispose of, which we did. It was a smell that has lived with me to this day.

Communication was difficult, although we managed to achieve regular conference calls with our French and American allies in Sarajevo. To ensure that we were properly co-ordinated, Jacko began a series of Joint Military Commissions for all the former warring factions to ensure compliance and issue orders for the next stage. He also travelled around the country to see and eyeball the commanders, with Elizabeta, his courageous and very able interpreter. I sometimes accompanied him and, after one particularly difficult encounter, he said, "Watch him, Freddie. I might just have to deal with him one day." I knew what he meant – this particular guy was devious and untrustworthy. I was sure he had blood on his hands and we might have to act so that he couldn't bother us or anybody else again. My guns were accurate enough to do that.

As winter dragged on, it occurred to me that, if we were called upon to fight, our soldiers had suffered from skill fade – they were 'ring rusty'; they needed more time to train – and our kit had taken a fair bashing during the deployment. If we were ordered to open fire, I wasn't completely sure that we would hit the target and we might injure innocent people in the process. Our tanks, guns, rifles and other weapons needed to be calibrated, but we had no range big enough to perform this safely. We had to find one before the spring allowed easier movement around the country. Such a facility would give us the added advantage of allowing us to demonstrate our capabilities to the former warring factions and give them a clear message: *Behave, or you will face the consequences. We are better armed, better trained and more determined than you are, so get the message.*

I was very lucky to have Major Nigel Linge in my team. He was a good man whom I knew from my time in 40 Regiment – a real professional and perfectly equipped to find and build me a range. He made a good plan and, after a little reluctance, the units in the multinational division all agreed to support our work. Nigel came back with a big smile: he had found an ideal place on the outskirts of a town called Glamoc. Most of the population had fled, houses were deserted and the real estate had everything we needed, with plenty of room and the capability of accommodating all our weapon systems and their danger areas. The area had been occupied by the Warsaw Pact forces and it had a purpose-built runway and buildings for its aircraft. I briefed Jacko. He was delighted with our work and told us to crack on. Ownership was easy; once I had found the local Croat Army Commander, Nic Glasnovic, and explained what I wanted, he agreed and gave me a signed document authorising me to carry on. I owned a range: lock, stock and – soon after we had made the necessary arrangements to open the place – plenty of smoking barrels. If we had to fire at something in anger, I reckoned we had a very good chance of hitting it. Nigel did us proud with his work on that. We came to use the range on an almost daily basis; Michael Portillo, the Secretary of State for Defence (with Margaret Aldred as his Private Secretary) came to see us and enjoyed his visit. He spent some time with the squadron from which two soldiers were killed driving over a mine during implementation of the peace agreement.

Our first base in Gornji Vakuf soon became impractical, without the space to accommodate us and a location too far to the south. We began to look for somewhere in the Serb Republic.

I knew of a place that had been occupied by Lieutenant Colonel Ben Barry of the Light Infantry. It was in a town called Banja Luka, the capital of the Serb Republic and, during the Cold War, it had been a huge metal factory some 600 yards long and 300 wide. It offered plenty of space for living, a headquarters that met our needs and room to base our helicopters and other life support. On a cold day with snow falling, I flew to the town and landed on their football pitch. The detachment of the SAS met me, the pilot said I had just a few hours before they would have to lift off to get home and avoid the impending snow storm, and we drove to the Serb Army Headquarters.

I met the commander and, like the weather, the reception was frosty to say the least. The Serb team there did not want to discuss or offer anything but, fortunately, I had the Dayton Agreement as my weapon and laid it on thick: it was their duty to provide us with some accommodation, immediately and without difficulty. Failure to do so would constitute non-compliance with what they had agreed. Time was passing and I had to leave to get back to the helicopter. I asked my interpreter to explain that the meeting was over, that the metal factory was what I wanted and, if not there, I expected an alternative by 1600 hours. I think they understood me me to say: "Banja Luka by 4pm, or else"! In any event, the phone rang and we got what we asked for: the metal factory in Banja Luka was ours, indefinitely. This was typical of the Serbs: they might play hard to get but they would come round in the end and deliver. As it turned out, the factory met our needs well and Jacko decided to move his Headquarters there. Colonel John Field, Commander of our Engineer Group, did a fantastic job in getting us in and it was to prove an excellent long-term solution.

Soon after we were settling in to our new Headquarters, we saw a stark reminder of very recent history. A German engineer battalion was tasked with repairing the roadways and bridges to improve access and mobility and could often be seen moving around the country. On one occasion, the battalion moved past the metal factory in convoy, wearing the helmets and displaying the well-known Iron Cross insignia on its armoured vehicles. It looked and sounded like the Wehrmacht. Hours later, hundreds of Bosnian people appeared outside the gates, demonstrating against the German deployment. We realised that this was all about recreating the memories that came from WW2 and we sent an interpreter out to meet the leader and reassure him that this was not an aggressive act, that the battalion was part of the Implementation Force structure and was working for Dayton. The demonstration was satisfied and went away but it showed how raw the memories were and how brittle confidence was in what we were doing.

The remainder of our tour passed off without major incident and, by the time we departed, Dayton was well established and, provided NATO kept a watchful eye, the stability of Bosnia Herzegovina was positive. We felt we had done a good job. Jacko returned to the UK and, soon after that, handed over command of his division to General Cedric Delves. I hoped that I would work for Jacko again one day; he had led us well and given us a hell of a ride. Morale was soaring and it felt good to be part of it.

Cedric was another cracking man to work for. He was a quietly spoken, tough and thoroughly professional soldier who, like Jacko, gave me a free hand. We visited Monte Cassino, Anzio and Rome with him and were visited quite often after our return from Bosnia. On one occasion, we were warned to host a senior general and commander of the Falklands Army on his first visit to the UK. He spoke little English so we planned his visit carefully. Cedric, himself a Falklands Veteran, came into our divisional briefing room to welcome him and told our team that they should not mention the Falklands War. The visitors' book was open and lay on the side table by the door. I looked at it and noticed that, directly above the book, was a painting of Sergeant Ian McKay winning his posthumous VC during the attack by 3 Para on Mount Longdon. I alerted Cedric. "Don't worry. He'll never see that," came the reply. Happily, he didn't.

My own experiences of Zagreb and Bosnia confirmed many of the frictions associated with operating in a multinational environment. The different contributing nations all had their own issues to consider, such as security policies, language, conflicting rules of engagement, new equipment and capabilities and different approaches to the task. It required a good deal of diplomacy to keep the nations' governments content and the Dutch, for example, were extremely nervous about a repeat of the Srebrenica scenario. Jacko devoted much of his time to visiting his units and the former warring factions, while General Mike Walker, the overall commander of the NATO Mission, put much of his focus on communicating and coordination. Thankfully, Dayton came to our aid on a number of occasions. Even in the benign environment that we faced in Bosnia, the effort we put in to keeping the place stable and maintaining confidence among a very bruised society was to serve us and me particularly well in the years ahead.

Jane handled my absence on our six month tour in Bosnia remarkably well. She had a really good and demanding job working for a well-known travel publisher and her boss, Martin Kenny, became a good friend and a regular, welcome guest in our home. Martin was later to leave the company and qualify at Law College in just two years, which was a great achievement. He became a barrister and was highly successful. Jane continued supporting Brendan and Kate while I was away, collecting them for regular weekends and holidays. On my return, we planned their combined 21st and 18th party at home in Bulford. Their many guests (our children limited us to six only) arrived on Saturday in dinner jackets and incredibly short dresses. One of

Kate's girlfriends appeared at the top of the stairs and asked me if I thought her dress was too short. I said it was fine. It wasn't. She became known as Tubigrip from then on and Bob Harmes was told by his wife, Pauline, to stop looking at her. Blippy (real name Luke), a friend of Brendan's, had far too much to drink and spent several hours wandering the party trying to force-feed leftover strawberries to us all. He was the last guest to leave, three days later, when we had run out of food and drink and told him to go home. Blippy was a pest but a very likeable lad.

As my two-year tour was coming to an end, my plan changed. I had been selected to attend the Royal College of Defence Studies in London. This was a prestigious one year course that studied the workings of defence at strategic level and provided world class speakers. I felt fortunate to be picked but, shortly afterwards, I was told that I would in fact not be attending RCDS but was to take on the role of Director of Manning for the Army. I was surprised but happy to get this change of post and it was only marred by having someone urging me to bring forward my handover date. This someone had been promoted and wanted me to fit in with his own plans, so that he could himself gain promotion and move on. He was unhappy to listen to my problem stemming from the short notice change (moving house, report writing and so on), and pulled rank to get his way. He was selfish and another example of the 'uplookers' I had come across. However, I agreed to the plan and he got his way.

Just as we were leaving that quarter, we found and bought a house in Hampshire. Jane started to transform it into our long-term home.

A NEW STRATEGY FOR PEOPLE

My move from 3rd division in 1996 to the Adjutant General Headquarters in Upavon as Director of Manning brought about a very steep learning curve in my education; like all postings I undertook, there were valuable lessons.

Within a few weeks, General Sir Michael Rose had been succeeded by Sir Alex Harley and he in turn faced a big challenge. During my handover, my predecessor once again appeared in an unseemly hurry to move on and we skirted around a range of complex problems without really looking at the solutions:

The Army was seriously undermanned and we didn't have enough people, by quantity or quality. Too many were leaving, too early.

We were recruiting well enough among troops from foreign and overseas nations but had no policy for how many we should have.

Our position on the selection, training and treatment of our female and ethnic minority recruits including non-UK was unclear and we faced assertions that our approach to discrimination was failing. The Equal Opportunities

Commission was after us and wanted to see improvement. Recruiting and employing females was a particular problem because the feeling at that time was that the job was better suited to males. We had no feel for how many ethnic minority soldiers would be a sustainable number for the duration of a career.

I wondered what I had taken on but, within the week, my predecessor left and it was my turn to try to do something to turn it around. It needed a lot of coffee and a lot more fag breaks!

Looking through the files, I came across a surprising piece of paper in the bottom drawer. It laid out the framework of an idea and proposed a way ahead. It talked about the introduction of a Human Resources Strategy, the current buzz word for 'people' and the fashionable phrase of the moment. *Marvellous*, I thought – *here's the answer!* It was news to me and, as I read on, I saw the difficulty with the idea: the proposal was not welcomed by my civil servant colleagues because it was too difficult, probably contentious and expensive and should not be pursued. A polite rejection from the MOD was parked and the file was left to gather dust.

But a little analysis showed that the strategy did indeed have some merit. This was the time of a Labour Government and the economy was struggling; all government departments were under pressure to make cuts and this had a direct effect on recruiting and retaining our soldiers. When the economy is weak, soldiers don't join up and they leave early. There is pressure on pay and conditions of Service life, including housing, training and equipment. Retention suffers. We were losing too many trained soldiers, our units were undermanned and struggling to meet operational demands. In contrast, a strong economy gives us the opportunity to make up for lost ground and put right some of the known weaknesses. It is a cyclical affair and we were at the bottom of the curve. I thought that there might be an opportunity here to identify what we needed to do and get it agreed before taking action. These things are rather like driving a super tanker; it takes a long time to turn the ship around and move off in a new direction.

I presented the case for the introduction of the Army's first HR Strategy to the AG's Management Committee and proposed a timetable to take it to the Army Board. It was met with a fair degree of scepticism, based I think on doing something differently and the cost implications of that, but I had a strong advocate in Michael Hockney, an experienced consultant with a great deal of management experience. He knew his stuff and, having got the committee's agreement to proceed, he became my key advisor, a strong ally and source of advice and encouragement. With his delightful wife Elizabeth, they became very good friends and remain so now. Over months, we examined the manning process in sequence, from recruiting, initial training, employment, retention and retirement. All angles were explored and we soon understood that motivation was a key element in attracting, keeping and supporting our soldiers and their families. And key to motivation was the offer, which we expressed as the Military Covenant; put simply, and best expressed by Sebastian Roberts, we said that, in return for our soldiers fulfilling the unlimited liability to go and do whatever was asked of them at any time for as long as necessary, we undertook to give them what they expected of us as good employers. This meant decent pay, decent equipment, decent training and decent housing. This statement was later to have profound implications and gain traction within Government. The financiers, of course, were always worried about cost.

Concurrent with developing the HR strategy, we were dealing with another tricky problem. Cuts and reductions to the overall size of the Army meant that we had to reduce our top structure and lose some senior officer ranks if the pyramid were to stay balanced and in a sustainable shape. This meant we needed to make our senior people redundant; it had to be done with dignity. It was a complicated business and it involved compensating someone who might want to stay. The Treasury would have a view, as would the MOD civilians and the Army Board. It needed a compelling case and, fortunately, I had a great ally inthe late Colonel Peter Daniel. Peter was a retired officer who knew the manning process backwards and he had an outstanding dedication to his task. He devised a plan called DER: Directed Early Retirement. Ably assisted by my deputy, Mark Mans, and by Richard Nugee, an officer of boundless enthusiasm and real ability, the DER paper was well argued, affordable and compelling and Peter did good work behind the scenes to get it accepted. He deserves great credit for that. A modest man, he loved his King Edward cigars and I enjoyed chatting to him at the end of the day about his Service life, his wife Alison and their talented family.

Eventually, we were ready to present our work on the strategy. Michael and I went on a series of visits with the senior leaders to gauge their reaction and pick up any observations. Some were very helpful indeed, and supportive, while others gave us more to think about. One working in the people domain actually said to me that if I thought I was going to be told all of his good ideas, I could think again. That struck me as coming from someone who was far too selfish and ambitious; he lost my trust and respect that day. As the process continued, he continued to be difficult and uncooperative. We ignored him.

Adjusting our approach and getting agreement to the strategy took time but we were soon ready to present our plans to the Army Board. Without the backing of the senior officers and financiers, we were going nowhere. Thankfully, the Adjutant General (and my boss) Alex Harley was fully supportive. The Army Board agreed to my paper. Michael Hockney and I were delighted; this was eighteen months of hard work and we were launched on to a new plan. I had learned more about the 'people' world than I thought I ever would. It proved to be an excellent education; I learned things that would prove invaluable when I later became Adjutant General.

At about this time, I received an invitation for Jane and me to attend a boxing match in aid of the Army Benevolent Fund: The Soldiers' Charity. The event had Jim Davidson as compère and world champion boxer John Conteh as prize giver. I had always enjoyed Jim's shows and John Conteh was my schoolboy hero. I was very keen to go but, as it didn't appeal to Jane at all, I invited our son Brendan to come along with me. It was a great night and I got along with Jim immediately. He was devoted to the Army and was already doing great work to support them. I hoped I might see him again but, typically, events got in the way. Our other guest at the boxing was Simon Weston and I was delighted to see that he was making a good recovery from his injuries in the Falklands campaign. Our paths would cross again later.

As the months passed, we continued to focus on delivering the strategy with a new team and whilst juggling the consequences of under-manning and poor retention. We had some success, but it was clear that we would be struggling for months before we would see any real improvement, particularly as the economy was still at a low.

And then came the good news. One Christmas, I took a surprise call from General Sir Roger Wheeler, the Head of the Army and a man with a phenomenal memory for names and places. He rang, he said, to wish me a Happy Christmas.

"Thank you, CGS."

"I have a present for you."

"Really?"

"Yes. You are going back to Bosnia. Next March. For a year. On promotion. Well done."

"Thank you, sir. Delighted."

Relief and a big surprise. This was an exciting prospect. I looked forward to commanding Multinational Division South West on familiar ground two years since I was there last. I began counting the days.

And what of the HR Strategy? My deployment to Bosnia prevented me from keeping track with its progress other than to see that it was to be replaced later by a second strategy, so the original had no time to settle down and begin to deliver benefits. Perhaps the strategy I took to the Army Board was seen as too difficult or expensive. I will never know. In any event, this second version was also done away with later and, by the time I became the Adjutant General, it no longer featured. But all was not lost as many lessons about recruiting, retention and conditions of Service were taken up.

My time as DM(A) was a valuable experience and taught me a lot about the workings of the Army Board and the MOD, the individuals involved and the challenges it faced. It would pay dividends later.

BOSNIA (REVISITED)

Returning to Bosnia in 1999 was rather different.

As Commander Multinational Division South West, I was responsible for an area about the size of Wales with some 8,000 men and women comprised of NATO nations from the Czech Republic, Belgium, Luxembourg, the Netherlands and the UK. Canada was there too in the form of the well-known Battalion of French origin, the 'Vin Doo', or 22nd. Two and a bit years since I was last there, my own Headquarters remained in the Banja Luka metal factory. The soldiers' facilities were improved but we still could not make a phone call home, our internet links were unreliable, there was nowhere to relax off duty and the pay structure was a mess. There were plenty of people-type issues to take on and improve. Thankfully, Colonel Stuart Cameron, my Deputy Chief of Staff who looked after welfare and people problems, saw it too and tackled his challenges head on with great enthusiasm.

My other great ally was my Political Advisor, Dr Richard Freer. He was an expert on the Serb political scene in Bosnia and had an instinctive feel for the impact of what we were planning to do. Softly spoken but with real authority, he was ever present at our briefings and key operational planning events and we would often talk late into the night about how the country was developing and what our reactions should be. The moment when the Russian contingent left the American command in Tuzla and took off for Kosovo was a particularly tense time. As Jacko explains in his account in *Soldier*, no-one really knew how things would turn out. I enjoyed Richard's company a lot.

Operationally, there was also a lot to think about. My previous boss, Jacko, was now in command of NATO's Allied Rapid Reaction Corps and working very hard trying to negotiate a peace deal with the Serbian army in Kosovo. For my part, I was surprised to find a group of twin-rotor Chinook helicopters on the helipad with 'KFOR – Kosovo Force' emblazoned on their tail rotors. *Interesting*, I thought; *last time I was here, our helicopters had 'SFOR – Stabilisation Force – on theirs.*

I rang Jacko.

"General, why you are nicking my helicopters?"

"Needs must, lad. Produce!" he replied.

I knew my place and why he needed them, so I did as he asked; I provided.

For me, keeping Bosnia calm unless and until Kosovo burst into flames was the most important thing I could do. Bosnia had had enough of the civil war and just wanted stability, but there were elements for whom it was not over; deterrence would be important. Lieutenant Colonel Patrick Marriott, commanding his Lancer Regiment, saw me soon after I arrived and advised me in the strongest terms to take his tanks away from their positions around the city. How, he argued, could I convince the Bosnians that, despite what I was saying, I could be trusted and wanted peace and security while they could see tanks everywhere? A very wise man. He was dead right, so the tanks were called home and we made other plans to deal with a disturbance among the crowd should a protest about Kosovo break out. I asked for help from the *Carabinieri* (Italian armed police) from Sarajevo and they came with their riot control vehicles, uniforms and smart sunglasses. I asked the team leader if he was happy to deal with an angry crowd in Banja Luka. "No problem," the Italian replied with a smile, "we're used to handling thousands of Roma fans most Saturdays in the football season."

Jacko's great work moved towards a peaceful resolution to the Kosovo crisis. The experience showed us that a sense of confidence through security was vital and, in Bosnia, we simply didn't have enough troops to cover the ground and be ready to intervene when required. We were covering the likely hot spots, but had nothing in reserve. So, we used the deployed troops as a framework, trouble-spotting force and kept a mobile reserve, ready to surge quickly where needed. Security, we decided, was the key to sustaining success and we inherited a good model for the purpose where key elements were assessed: the programme of refugee returns; weapon collection; employment opportunities; illegal activity including theft, the smuggling of huge logs cut down from the forests covering the high ground and drugs. This showed us where we needed a presence and for how long, and it gave us the opportunity to run an information campaign to reassure the local people about why we were there and what we were doing. For this, I was well served by having a local FM radio station in the factory, able to reach almost the whole of the country and give the people a type of BBC2 radio station: popular music with local news. Our radio coordinator was a real enthusiast and we were able to find him a better site, send his programme team back to the UK for training with the BBC and learn how to plan good programmes. On one occasion, we invited Mr Graham Hand, the UK's Ambassador in Bosnia, to join us for a phone discussion. The result was extraordinary; we had enough people wanting to ask him questions to fill the programme countless times. It showed the real hunger for information.

During our travels to spread the word, I had a key player with me; Elizabeta, my courageous, loyal and resilient interpreter, who once worked for Jacko. My old Regiment, 3 RHA, were also based there at the time and my excellent ADC, Captain Richard Clements, came to join me. He planned and arranged a comprehensive monthly visit plan. Elizabeta supported me on many of my trips by car and helicopter to the outlying towns and villages, meeting the community leaders and military commanders. Her commitment was extraordinary and, despite the risks we were taking, she remained cheerful throughout, enjoying the banter with my drivers and close protection team (who called her my 'interrupter'). She had a great sense of humour and took no nonsense from them. She was fun to have around. I owe her and Miryjana, her colleague, a lot.

During my ten-month tour, my daily routine rarely changed. The working day would start with a thirty-minute daily brief at 08:00, when we would hear about the events of the previous evening, covering intelligence, operations, logistics, personnel issues and the programme for the coming day. Occasionally, I would give some direction on what I had heard but this was rare as I had such a strong and competent team around me. I would then depart on my visit programme or prepare for any inbound visitors, which included: politicians; NATO's Supreme Allied Commander, General Wes Clark; my American operational commander in Sarajevo (General Monty Meigs, who can trace his direct family history back to the Civil War in the nineteenth century); and the occasional visitor from the MOD or the media. Travelling the length and breadth of my patch in Bosnia was still a dangerous business so, weather permitting, the helicopter was always first choice and by the end, I had completed around 500 hours flying in Lynx, Chinook and the Canadian UH47. I was especially grateful to my favourite and regular Lynx pilot, Staff Sergeant Hay of the Royal Tank Regiment, for his great skills. Flying was a difficult business and it took a great deal of planning to find the right route and to know how to escape and get back if the weather turned nasty. He had to be familiar with the many pylon lines in the country, which had often turned rusty and were almost invisible against the forests in the steep valleys, and be aware of the aircraft's capabilities. He would often say to me, "If there's any doubt, there's no doubt," and I never argued. Hay was a good soldier. He turned me into something of a flying addict.

I would always plan to be back in the Headquarters by 18:00 in time for the evening update, run by my highly efficient ADC Richard (not a fan of flying). This brought me up to speed with the events of the day in time for my video conference call with General Mike Willcocks, my overall boss in Sarajevo. My American and French counterparts, based respectively in Tuzla and Mostar, outlined the key events of the day and we would hear about what Sarajevo was planning. It was a good session when communications allowed and kept us commanders aware of what was happening across the country.

We did our best to keep weekends as free from essential duties as possible. Occasionally, Richard and I would travel to a wonderful villa, overlooking the bay near Split in Croatia, for a planning conference with my French and American fellow commanders, but mostly Saturday was when my command team assembled to think ahead and talk about where best to focus our attention in the coming weeks. We didn't interfere too much with the deployed units as they needed some time to themselves for recreation and administration. Sunday tended to be a quiet time when I attended the 1000 church service and met some colleagues for coffee afterwards.

Walking one Sunday with Colonel Ian Tritton, we saw a

young soldier coming towards us. He was clearly very busy, striding quickly along the corridor between the machines. The metal factory is a huge space and, with the bright sun in his face, he clearly hadn't spotted us. Ian and I made room for him and he walked straight between us.

"Stand still, young man," said Ian. The soldier stopped and turned to face us. "We have a tradition in the British Army. We salute each other. On this occasion, you go first."

He looked at me, saw my rank and saluted smartly. I returned the compliment.

"Well done. Now please, carry on."

"Sorry, sir," he said and walked away even more quickly.

"Shall we continue?" said Ian with a smile. Good man!

In the afternoon, I liked to get away from the metal factory and visit a place where I hadn't been for a while to see how the local community was getting along. The village of Prynjavor was a favourite spot because it was the home of the Lipizzaner horses, used by the Spanish Riding School in Vienna; one of only three places where the famous white horse is bred and trained.

With that routine, my time there passed very quickly and I thoroughly enjoyed my command tour. The men and women for whom I was responsible were always keen and enthusiastic because they were properly commanded, manned and equipped and had clear objectives. Discipline was rarely a big issue. I saw the same thing in Iraq and Afghanistan later on and it was quite a contrast, knowing how much the rest of the Army was struggling to meet its demands while being understaffed and overcommitted. In my later appointments, I saw time and again that it is highly cost efficient if our political and bureaucratic masters can get 80% of our Service men and women to do 100% of the work and ignore the complaints from the chain of command. People are the Army's most precious resource; taking them for granted and ignoring the warning signs has hidden and unwelcome consequences.

Three aspects of this time stick in my memory.

First is my trip to Rome, where I met Jane to enjoy our rest and recuperation break. We had a long standing plan to travel there after my previous visits and we were determined to go for a week in May, provided, of course, that the situation would allow that. Kosovo remained tense as Milosevic had not yet conceded. We booked the Hotel d'Anselmo on one of Rome's seven hills. It had a stunning view of the Vatican, overlooking the city. We had a wonderful week in glorious weather together, travelling to all the famous sites, people-watching over coffee (my favourite sport, or at least a close second to rugby) and enjoying the local restaurants. All too soon, our stay came to an end and I returned to Bosnia. The country was still there and remarkably quiet, which was good news for me.

Secondly, our operation began to give the people a sense that the war really was over and that it was time to rebuild the ravaged country. The future depended on it. Key to this was the plan to clear the place of its redundant weapons, some of which dated back to WW2. As part of the information campaign, we carried on with and re-energised Operation 'Zetva', or Harvest, a plan to clean up Bosnia. The result was extraordinary and we removed literally thousands of guns, explosives and ammunition from homes, farm buildings and factories. The population came out in droves and it showed that the local people really had had enough of the war and wanted to get rid of what they were hiding. The death of Corporal Bradley of the Royal Engineers, blown up when a hand grenade he was examining exploded in front of him, was an isolated tragedy within the otherwise successful exercise. It made us all feel incredibly sad (by chance, I arrived on the scene less than half an hour after it happened). Brigadier Nick Parker commiserated with me over a whisky in the evening and told me that, whatever I thought, we could not stop this important work. He was right. We returned to the Croatian port and airhead at Split with his regimental escort, mourned the loss of Brad, observed his repatriation service, and carried on with the operation.

The third aspect that sticks was the pursuit and apprehension of war criminals, a key mission for me and the International Criminal Tribunal based in The Hague. The UK had a good record here but we could not relax. It was important to show the people of Bosnia that we were determined to root out those accused of war crimes and bring them to justice. Those indicted came from witness statements, which were taken from refugees and those returning at the end of the civil war, about the prison guards and commanders in the concentration camps in the Serb-held areas around Banja Luka of Prijedor, Keraterm and Trnopolje, often widely photographed and well publicised. Evidence taken from the Bosnian and Muslim population alleged torture, starvation, punishment and murder. Acts of genocide were a frequent claim. Most of those accused of war crimes were Serbs and lived around Banja Luka.

I was fortunate to have a highly capable team in the Headquarters, dedicated to the task of hunting these individuals, getting positive identification, tracking their pattern of life and, eventually, conducting their capture and arrest. These criminals knew they were being hunted and went to some lengths to hide their identity in the attempt to avoid capture. It required really good intelligence, patience and determination to conduct operations without detection. I visited the team often to keep up to date, understand their activities and know the places they wanted me to avoid to prevent the target from seeing me and trying to escape. These soldiers were a highly impressive bunch.

During one briefing, I was told that my arrest team had just returned from downtown Banja Luka. They had been tracking a known criminal and thought he was parked outside the Serb Government offices. We had to have a positive ID before we could conduct a hasty, no-notice arrest so, as the team prepared to deploy, an armed covert operator moved off to confirm the identity. Spotting the car, he saw the man inside and conducted the walk past, reached the individual and looked down. He saw that the man was wearing a wristwatch that didn't match the known profile so, uncertain, called off the arrest and the team returned. It showed the need for patience as we could not afford a wrongful arrest. It was the right decision.

The precise time and place of the arrest was a tense period. Having established the pattern of life and planned the arrest, I then had to get the permission from my Headquarters in Sarajevo to proceed. Armed with that, I gave the green light and we then went into the essential need-to-know phase; only those directly involved knew about our plans, the place was cleared of anyone who might blunder into our area and arouse suspicion. After the arrest was over, my task then was to get around my multinational partners and let them know what had happened, if they were affected, and visit the mainly Serb Government Headquarters to brief the minister on the effect of what we had done. Keeping it quiet from the MOD was also difficult; we had a good record of arrests among our NATO partners and the civil servants would enjoy crowing about what the UK had done. I once threatened to sack one of them if he dared to send the e-mail out early, before we had the man safely in custody. He had done it before and almost compromised our operation through his desire to be the first to report an arrest. He didn't do it again.

As the months progressed, we arrested four men successfully. The last was part of the Serbian War Council triumvirate – one of the top three within the command structure, well into his sixtieth year, a bit frail and a very high-profile target indeed.

As we were about to move out, I said to the team leader, "You're not going to hurt him, are you?"

"No boss," he said, "unless he doesn't come out of the car fast enough."

His arrest went well and he was brought back to my headquarters to be guarded pending his flight back to The Hague. By law, I had just a few hours to get him into custody or, failing that, I had to release him. That night, Murphy intervened. It was December and the country had the biggest snowfall on record. Everything was cut off, rail and road links were inoperable and we went into movement shut down to avoid unnecessary risks to life and limb. Fortunately, communications worked and, when the weather allowed, we took a look at Banja Luka airport. It was being cleared to allow flights in and out. I kept ringing Sarajevo to tell them what was happening and how many hours we had left, urging them to fly into my airport and let me get the prisoner to the aircraft and back to The Hague. Eventually, the plan was agreed and we got our man away; we had made the deadline – but it was a very close run thing. Relief all round and, as the snow continued to fall, we went into survival mode, limiting movement to essential trips only.

At the end of 1999, our minds turned to the effects of the millennium and whether our IT support would be affected as 2000 arrived. The possible impact could have been serious indeed and affect our ability to communicate and conduct operations safely. Thankfully, as the dates changed at midnight, there was no effect at all. "No fuss," said Ian Tritton. "The only chips we have in this place are in the restaurant."

After ten months, and as my tour came to an end, I heard that my successor was to be Major General Robin Brims, whom I had last seen on the dockside at Ploce, Croatia in 1995. I knew he would be an ideal man to replace me and would carry on strengthening the foundations we had built. As for me? I was told that I had been selected to become the Chief of Staff at the Army's major Headquarters at Wilton near Salisbury. My boss, the Commander in Chief, was to be Jacko. I was delighted with this opportunity to work with him again and I knew that it would be an exciting time, as we juggled the demands of operational commitments, financial pressures and bureaucratic processes.

I left Bosnia with some wonderful memories of truly impressive people, including Brigade Commanders Riley, Cook, Parker and Cooper and an American Reservist, Ben Lucas. Ben was a highly experienced Attorney, sent to advise the Bosnian Government in Sarajevo on the legal issues of constructing a government. He lived with us in the metal factory and I got to know him and, later, his wife Barbara, well. They lived in Baltimore and Florida and, once Barbara retired, they would visit Europe and the UK frequently. We would enjoy meeting them and hearing about their adventures, particularly Ben's sailing trips and Barbara's role in escorting HRH The Prince of Wales on his visit to the United States to see Mount Vernon, President George Washington's home. Very kind and generous folks and fun to be with.

The Brigade Commanders gave me their support and made a difference to the ongoing stability of the country. Command of the Multinational Division was a thoroughly enjoyable time, but it demonstrated once again the challenges faced by a structure like this. I saw many of the issues facing us from our first time there and realised that the contributing NATO nations' eyes were on us. On one occasion, while visiting our Czech Battalion, I was asked to speak directly to their Defence Minister and reassure him that his forces would not be withdrawn as part of the reductions planned by the UK. I did. On another, I took a call from a very senior member of the Belgian Government and was rebuked for deploying one of the battalion's platoons into the town of Prozor, to maintain a presence over the mainly

Croat community, without prior authority. It showed the powerful extent of the effects of recent events of Srebrenica on the political psyche.

As I write this, there is talk about forming a European Army in the context of the UK's withdrawal from the European Union. Despite how attractive this might appear, we need to be wary of it. In my experience of operating in Bosnia, trying to pull together and build a multinational structure is very unwise. Working effectively, even in a benign environment, is extremely difficult. Conducting offensive operations against a hostile force to achieve a political end is virtually impossible. It is a notion that should be resisted at every turn.

Wherever I went, I found soldiers who were enjoying their jobs and getting on without complaint, regardless of the sometimes difficult operating conditions. Why? It is because the soldiers and units that deploy to these places usually go at full strength, with equipment that works and a functioning supply system. They know their tasks, morale is high, discipline is good and complaints are few. I have seen circumstances on operations where that happy situation did not apply and witnessed the frustration on the faces of many who knew what to do but simply did not have the tools to do it. Ignoring the effects of all this risks mission failure and I sometimes wish that visitors to operational theatres would listen more to what commanders are reporting. If they are found to be exaggerating, remove them. Otherwise, trust them. Putting the Armed Forces' lives at risk unnecessarily is just not acceptable.

As I came home, I suffered some real withdrawal, post-command symptoms and, on reflection, I should have taken Jane away on a holiday to relax and recover. But for various reasons, I didn't. Bosnia was a fantastic experience but it came at a cost and I learnt my lesson. Ignoring my wife was selfish and I should not have done it. Thankfully, we came out of it and we were ok.

My other regret from my time in Bosnia was that I did not receive an annual Confidential Report (CR) about my performance there. I asked for one from my operational boss frequently as my tour came to an end but it never appeared. Eventually, I gave up. It was a pity because the CR is the only record of my achievements in Bosnia that is missing from my report book (a statement of performance set against key tasks and responsibilities for the year; assessment of potential for promotion; recommendations for future employment). I had no reason to expect the CR to be critical or limiting about me but it could have been and I will never know. Thankfully, Jacko spotted this some years later and I explained my difficulty. He corrected the error in my report book immediately to set the record straight. But I never did see a copy of the CR.

JACKO

I arrived at Wilton in early 2000 to become Chief of Staff to the United Kingdom's Land Forces (UKLF), then called Land Command, supporting my Commander in Chief, Jacko – soon to be General Sir Mike Jackson. He was to join us shortly, so I used my time to get around the Command with Major Craig Lawrence, my highly impressive Military Assistant, to meet the bosses and find out what was needed; it was really a recce.

The command consisted of two deployable divisions (1 and 3), numbering about 55,000 troops, trained and ready to go wherever ordered and supported by a regional structure in Germany and the UK. The regions were also responsible for supporting the nation at time of need; natural, man-made or otherwise. The Army's reserve component, the TA, had a critical role here as well, being prepared and trained to bring the divisions up to the required strength in time of crisis. At home, the pressure was on to make savings through so called 'efficiency measures' by bureaucrats who knew the cost of everything and value of nothing. It was rather like a game where arguments about preserving the Army's operational effectiveness made little difference and the effects of cuts were largely hidden. I would see the impact of these cuts on the soldiers and their families later on.

As I completed my recce, it became clear that, while the deployable divisions were well led and supported and had no major concerns to take back to the Headquarters, the regional commands were weak, essentially because the command structure was wrong. The regions had no-one to provide direction at the top, so the 'robber barons' (senior officers who commanded regional headquarters in a semi-autonomous way, without a superior commander, and so had no direction or control of their activities) were allowed to follow their own agenda largely unchallenged and argue their case to meet their ends. It stood out as a shortcoming. In the words of my good and wise friend Michael Hockney, from my time as Director of Manning, the 'machinery' was wrong and, over time, it would cause us to struggle.

Jacko arrived fresh from his time bringing peace and stability to Kosovo and we began to brief him on his new role as the force provider (as opposed to force user) to meet the Government's demands. I said that, while the deployable divisions were in good heart and had few concerns, the regional structure needed attention. It was unwieldy and I recommended he allow me to continue with a fundamental review that had been started by his predecessor. I said that, while there was no appetite to create new senior posts, any additions we needed had to be found from reductions elsewhere – and I thought we could and had to do that. Jacko saw the logic immediately and told me to crack on. Project LANDMARK was born and it was to consume most of our time in the early months as we worked to prepare a convincing case. Brigadier David Bill was the officer responsible for the project in the Headquarters and he set to it with a will.

Jacko's command style was ideal: he left me to get on with running the Headquarters day to day and expected me to let him know when I needed direction. He could see to the heart of a complex issue easily and identify what needed to be done with great clarity. I would do my best to think about all the questions he might ask and invariably he would ask one I hadn't anticipated. He had steel, too, and we would enjoy a frank discussion, usually over a cigar or cigarette and a whisky and soda. In short, he was a fabulous boss and I looked forward to going to work every day.

During the summer of 2000 Jane and I began to plan our leave holiday and decided that we wanted to go back to France. We had been there twice before and enjoyed our stay along the Dordogne river valley. France is a delightful country with a very relaxed attitude to life. It did me good to practise my French during our regular shopping trips and paddling downstream in the sunshine along the river was a peaceful way to spend the day. Paddling back was certainly more of a physical workout. We knew the towns of Sarlat, Souillac and Dom well and liked to visit the ancient cave drawings at Lascaux. We found a pretty farmhouse in the village of La Cipiere and booked it for a two week break. There was plenty of room in the cottage and we asked Brendan, just back from university, if he would like to ask Rebecca Goddard to join us. He had no girlfriend then and we had long admired Becky – a classmate of his from Kings' College – as an attractive, positive and capable girl. They had become good friends at school and we thought they would make a great couple. Becky accepted the invite and we watched and hoped as we all enjoyed a great holiday in near-perfect sunshine.

Brendan and Becky returned from holiday and soon became an item. They married in 2003 and Becky accused us of arranging the whole thing. We denied it – but she was right. We're delighted with the outcome.

Our task in support of the Civil Ministry was tested at short notice as we were called upon to intervene on behalf of the government in the latest crisis; the outbreak of the foot and mouth in early 2001. The Government panicked as more and more animals across the country were found to be infected. Inoculation wasn't possible, so slaughter was the only answer and the media showed some very distressing images of whole herds of cattle and sheep, killed and piled up for burning. The farmers suffered by far the most as disease spread like wildfire around the country. As a pretend farmer in my childhood, I had bags of sympathy for them.

In Cumbria, Brigadier Alex Birtwhistle, a straight-talking Lancastrian, was deployed to coordinate the relief effort. This came as no surprise to us; we knew that it had happened some fifty years before and that, back then, the Army was called in to support. We retrieved the Post Operation report and its key recommendation was very helpful. It advised us to get a competent headquarters deployed as soon as possible to advise the authorities. We sent this up to the MOD and began to think about who to call on. Typically, the Ministry of Agriculture and Fisheries (MAFF) were highly reluctant to ask but, eventually, the pressure told and the request arrived. Brigadier Malcolm Wood, a very able logistician, was sent with his team and he had to work hard to win the confidence of the Ministry's civilians; most of those working there had no idea of what the Army could do for them. Eventually, the disease was halted and we were called back, leaving thousands of farmers to deal with the challenge of rebuilding their lives and livelihoods without animals. Alex, seen as the saviour of the day, was left to deal with the trauma of shattered families for years afterwards. Plagued by the media, who saw the disease as the latest crisis facing the Government and revelled in telling the story, Alex had to devote too much of his time correcting the errors. As he so rightly said, "Rumours get round the world before the truth puts its boots on." Getting the story right is a good lesson to learn. Sadly, I lost touch with Alex soon after he retired but I hope that he hadn't found the experience too difficult. He was a good man.

As the year went on, we were increasingly called upon to intervene in other industrial disputes. Jacko said we did all the Fs – foot and mouth, fire, floods, fuel. I told him it was a good thing the Royal Mail weren't on strike – we could call it philately. Project Landmark went well and we were ready to present our case to tighten our command structure, create a new post from savings elsewhere and change our working processes. By this stage, Brigadier David Bill had become an expert in the field and made a compelling case for change, but there was no certainty that the MOD would back our recommendations. Finally, David came in to my office and gave me the good news (as it happened, on my birthday): we had got what we asked for. It was an ideal present and we felt the benefits straight away. The 'robber barons' were put back in their box and a new commander turned the telescope on the regional command structure. Landmark worked and we were better placed to take on the bureaucrats over the inexorable fight for resources, to deliver high-quality training and provide for the soldiers and their families.

The next couple of years brought about two key events.

For the first time since the Kosovo crisis, Jacko was invited to go to the Serbian capital of Belgrade, the first senior officer to be asked. The programme ran over two days and I accompanied his Military Assistant, Lieutenant Colonel Mark Carleton Smith, and Mike Venables, a senior civil servant in the Wilton Headquarters who had been with Jacko in Kosovo as his political advisor. As we worked on the programme, we decided that the key part of the trip was to get the Serb Government to hand over Milosevic, a man indicted as a war criminal from the civil war; redevelopment funding to rebuild a city badly damaged in the Kosovo bombing depended on his arrest. We hammered this message home with everyone we met in the Government's ministerial offices but with little prospect of a successful outcome. Our last chance at this came with a dinner hosted by our Ambassador with the Serbian Army's High Command present. They were a pretty surly bunch, didn't say much over dinner and left early with the Milosevic message in their ears.

It was early so, as Jacko and I were going upstairs, I remembered that there was a bottle of whisky in my room, so I suggested one for the road. He agreed and we sat on his veranda on a warm summer's evening and talked very late into the night. Eventually, we turned in and Jacko asked me to get him up in time for his live interview on national TV that morning. Fortunately, I always carried an alarm clock in my bags, so we made the deadline – just. Jacko's interview was spot on but I wished that I had gone to bed earlier than I did.

Carleton Smith and Venables saw me that morning, smiled and said, "You look knackered."

"Thanks," I said; they were right but the flight home later that day helped me sleep. Belgrade was a great visit.

The second event was to change the course of history forever. Attending a meeting in Upavon on 11 September, a young officer came in and showed the Chairman a picture of an aircraft flying in to the Twin Towers in New York. Moments later, he came in again: a second plane had also flown into the second building. My neighbour at the meeting, the Director of the UK's Special Forces group, said, "That's no accident. That's Al Qaeda. See you." He left and I didn't see him again for another year. The meeting adjourned and we returned as fast as possible to our Headquarters, during which time a further aircraft was flown into the Pentagon and another crash landed in Pennsylvania. It was clear to us that nothing would be the same after those horrific events.

Brigadier Roger Brunt, working at Wilton and responsible for the Army's overall operational and support tasks, was a trusted ally and ran our Commitments team; he did a great job sending troops to London to protect our vulnerable points in a hurry: "Move now. Orders to follow." Jacko was visiting troops exercising in Canada at the time and we made contact on the prairie. I explained over a crackly phone what we knew and had seen; his reaction was clear: "I'm in the wrong place. I need to return." I told him to get back to Calgary airport while we tried to find a flight home. It was going to be difficult: nations were closing their airspaces everywhere and aircraft were being sent home or allowed only to carry on to their destination. In the US, there was tension everywhere as we tried to make sense of what we could do. Fortunately, there was an aircraft at the airport being prepared to bring some casualties home. We got authority for Jacko to get aboard and he had an eerie flight, being escorted by fighter aircraft out of Canadian airspace and then having no communication with any air control authority until our aircraft reached the UK. He reached the airport safely and I was glad to see him home. I needed direction at what was going to be a difficult time, knowing that the UK would play a key part in the international effort to deal with these murderers.

It soon became clear that President Bush was determined to defeat what he described as 'the axis of evil'. Al Qaeda (AQ) had gone into hiding in the Tora Bora mountains of Afghanistan; Osama Bin Laden, AQ's leader, was thought to have escaped into Pakistan. That and Saddam Hussein's regime in Iraq were the key priority targets. The British Prime Minister, Tony Blair, was determined to support Bush in his efforts and there followed a period of frantic diplomacy as the UK gained authority to go to war in pursuit of Weapons of Mass Destruction (WMD). There was an unseemly battle as the three Services wanted to be involved. The RAF had a clear role, the Navy were desperate to be included in the force that would be sent, whether or not there was a clear role for them. This was typical of their behaviour at the time; their flag had to be on the map somehow and, at briefings at our headquarters in Northwood, it was clear that the Army's role had not been defined beyond the fact that there would be a task for a brigade if not a division somewhere.

I came back and told Jacko that, for the first time, I was nervous of how things were turning out. He told me to keep making the case and that common sense would prevail. He was right, of course and, eventually, General Robin Brims, with the 1st Armoured Division, was committed to the fight. Fortunately, Robin had recently returned from an exercise in the Middle East and his brigades had learned a good deal about desert warfare and were well worked up. As we began planning in earnest, everybody wanted a slice of the action and I got pestered by a number of irritating 'medal hunters' looking to get involved. I arranged with Major General Rob Fry, the Chief of Staff at the Permanent Joint Headquarters at Northwood, that I would not deploy anyone without his prior knowledge and authority, so that he could control who was involved and the numbers going. He helped me temper the over-enthusiasm and ambitions of some.

Eventually, the green light was given and so began the 2003 Iraq War. The US Army's performance in the early days was stunning and Robin did a great job. Baghdad fell, the Saddam Regime crumbled and the honeymoon period began. Soon after the start of the war, Jacko had moved on from Wilton to become the Chief of the General Staff (CGS). I had had three marvellous years with him and my other ally, Cedric Delves, and said that I felt like I was grieving. Jacko knew that I wasn't exactly ecstatic about his successor; his man-management and leadership style was so different.

"Best to get on with it lad. You'll be OK," he said.

Shortly afterwards, CGS asked me to check a revised command structure, showing a Major General to act as Senior British Military Representative for Iraq and Deputy Commander for the US-led Coalition. I'd seen a similar plan work well in

Bosnia and told Jacko I wanted the job. He told me to leave it with him, got me the job and told his replacement that I was to go. He also told me to be back by September to be ready for my next job. Jane reminded me that Brendan was getting married in the summer of 2003. She told me to get back for that, or stay in Iraq and don't come back. Crystal clear!

So I left Wilton with some fond memories of good people, especially my Military Assistants, Craig, Simon and Rob, and Pam, my ever loyal PA. I would miss them.

My three years as Jacko's Chief of Staff were hard work but very rewarding. He had the confidence to let me run the Headquarters and rarely interfered with what I was doing. His direction was clear and I trusted his judgement completely. The interests of his soldiers were at the heart of his thinking and he knew what mattered. We have kept in touch since and enjoyed many good lunches together.

IRAQ & THE INQUIRY

In early 2003, we flew into Kuwait to meet my predecessor, Major General Albert Whitley, and begin the handover. Experts were assembling in the form of General Tony Pigott, whom I knew from my very first tour in the MOD; John Sawers, a key player in the US/UK coalition political and military effort; and people from Prime Minister Tony Blair's office, whom I did not meet.

Sometime later, we took the flight from Kuwait to Baghdad airport and I enjoyed the view of the country from the flight deck of an RAF Hercules aircraft. Flying over the Euphrates river valley was like a scene from biblical times; a river flowing across the desert with small fishing boats, reed beds and oxen grazing among the strips of green woodland and palm trees near the banks. It was a memorable sight but the damage done by Saddam was obvious. He had built dams to prevent the water supplies from irrigating the land and so starve out the Shia population.

Our descent into Baghdad International airport was exciting, to say the least. The aircrew were aware of the threat from surface-to-air missiles against the Hercules (a hit would have killed all of us), so we descended rapidly from high altitude onto the runway and moved quickly to the holding area. The sky was clear and, even in the evening, it was hot and airless. A couple of Land Rover Discoveries ('Discos') were there and I met my staff and close protection team, including Staff Sergeant Primrose (Prim), Corporal Rob Bartrum of the Royal Military Police, and Sergeant Frank Spencer in the RAF Police. They were highly capable lads and I knew from my time in Bosnia – where I had a very similar set up – that they would look after me, provided I listened to Frank. Frank didn't smile much.

My civil/military team from the UK were a good, capable bunch and I could see that Albert had looked after them well. My officers had come through a testing time and were pleased to have reached their objective. My political advisor, Richard, was a civil servant from the MOD and another highly experienced man. Travelling into Baghdad on one occasion, Richard asked my close protection team why he kept being called "Chaff". Frank replied, "Because you will be the first to get thrown out if we have to leave in a hurry. That's why."

Throwing our kit in the back, we took the thirty minute drive from the airport to the Headquarters of the US Corps Coalition Forces close to the airport and occupied our accommodation inside a huge palace overlooking a stinking lake used by Saddam to host and entertain visitors. The ostentation was obscene: chandeliers under a huge dome, imitation French antique furniture in the rooms, evidence of the ruling Ba'ath party everywhere and fake gold in the washrooms. The only things missing were hot water and windows; the dust storm that night left everything covered in sand.

In the morning, we started to clean up and look around. The accuracy of the US military's 'Shock and Awe' tactics had done serious damage to the palace but it was still standing and we made ourselves as comfortable as possible, prioritising health and hygiene. Drinking safe water and eating the Americans' unpleasant ration packs ('MREs' – Meals Ready to Eat) kept us going. Laundry was OK because we at least had cold water for showers and the heat would dry out the washing within a few minutes, so we felt we could get along.

The following day we moved into Baghdad city and met my senior command team in Saddam's Palace, a twenty minute drive from the airport. The overall commander, General Dave McKiernan, introduced his team. They had come through a stunning operation and here we were, in Baghdad some twenty days after the advance from Kuwait began. The Americans had planned on that stage taking a hundred days. The 'shock' bit worked. We had our first meeting with the former warring factions to outline who the Coalition Forces were, our intentions as far as the rebuild was concerned (especially power and oil), how we fitted in with the civilian agencies, and our wish that their heavy weapons should be handed in. Their reaction was hostile; we were told that it would not happen overnight. I also met some of my coalition operational commanders in the regions. Impressive men: US Generals David Patreaus in Mosul, Ray Odierno in Tikrit, Scott Wallace in Baghdad, Marty Dempsey, a major general commanding the American 1st Armoured division in Baghdad. Marty later went on to assume the post of Chairman of the Joint Chiefs of Staff, the highest US military post in the Pentagon.

It soon became clear that living at the airport and driving at least twice a day into Saddam's Palace and the coalition headquarters in Baghdad city was too risky for all of us. The dual carriageway into the city was hot, dusty and busy with Iraqis in dangerous cars and trucks who had no respect for the rules of safe driving. Sudden lane changing, braking and overtaking were a common habit. The risks of a serious crash were a daily occurrence and my two cars used some effective counter measures to reduce the likelihood. Checkpoints were guarded by American troops using tanks for protection and meant we travelled in uniform with UK flags prominent on the cars. This made us stand out to anyone watching us moving about and also increased the threat of ambush. We were on borrowed time. Prim once came very close to shooting an armed Iraqi but stopped when he saw that this was just celebratory fire by a gang in a car. We realised that we had to do something different and my team started to recce a new place. They found an ideal spot – a very large house with plenty of space next to the river and inside the safe 'green zone' where routine travel was protected. It was perfect for our requirements but was already occupied by a US engineer battalion. I explained our needs to General Scott Wallace, who agreed to my request immediately and said I could have it. This was typical of the Americans' generosity and determination to look after the Brits well.

The resident US engineer battalion cleaned up for us and were gone within thirty-six hours, letting us move in at our leisure. Coincidentally, Albert Whitley and I had visited the Commonwealth War Cemetery in the city and were shown around by a disabled Iraqi who had tended the place throughout Saddam's reign of terror. Hidden among the graves was a mausoleum marking where a British officer, General Frederick Maude, was buried. He had commanded the Commonwealth force in Mesopotamia in the early 1900s which suffered thousands of casualties from all over the world. He himself died of cholera in 1917. We decided that his memory needed preserving, so my new quarters became known as Maude House.

After introducing me to the US Ambassador Paul (Jerry) Bremer, the civilian head of the Coalition Provisional Authority, or CPA, it soon became time for Albert to leave. He and I drove from Baghdad to Basra in southern Iraq, a journey of about six hours via the famous religious site of the Ziggaret of Ur, to say farewell. Albert had done a great job and, as we took a boat trip around Basra Harbour, I hoped I could live up to his legacy. As Albert left, it soon became time for Lieutenant General Dave Mckiernan to hand over to General Ric Sanchez, who was to work closely with Jerry Bremer in rebuilding the political, economic and security structures, all of which were broken. Ric was an extremely hard-working officer with a gracious and generous heart and really understood how to command soldiers. Meanwhile, Dan Haan (his Chief of Staff) had a punishing work routine and I hoped he could sustain it in the months ahead.

My job was to act as Ric's deputy commander, working with the civilian agencies to see how best the military could help to contribute. My UK boss, General John Reith, was always ready to take a call and give advice. As ordered by General Sir Mike Walker – the Chief of Defence Staff (CDS) – I submitted a report twice a week to John Reith and the Secretary of State (SofS) for Defence, outlining the political, economic and security headlines and any key issues to follow up. Typically, this report found its way not to the offices of the SofS and CDS but to the senior civil servant briefer on Iraq; he clearly hated surprises and wanted to get his perspective in first. So I then started to send mine to Jacko as Chief of the General Staff, so that he could also see what I was saying. Anything that really worried me could be aired confidentially at our weekly video links back to the UK with all the experts there. I had a fall back if I needed it and I often used it to ensure that the real story got through.

However, I had to be careful with what I said. The CPA did not want to hear bad news and any suggestion of criticism would not be well received. This got worse as the temperature increased and situation deteriorated and it was important for me to employ as much diplomacy as possible to keep the ship on an even keel. I found that the Brits quite enjoyed criticising the Americans, particularly the way they were conducting counter-insurgency operations. Hearing visitors say, "When I was in Northern Ireland" time and again became frustrating and I could tell that the US military did not want to hear it either. They had a war-fighting culture and way of working. They did not see building the peace as their concern and they were not equipped to do it. My weekly reports and video conferences helped a lot here but, on reflection, I wish that I had made more of a fuss about what I was seeing going on around me. I guess I might have been sent home if I did; I did not see that as my role and it wouldn't have helped anyway.

I took the time to get to know the main players, such as the United Nations and its High Commission for Refugees. I met Sergio de Mello when he arrived to work alongside Jerry Bremer and I liked him immediately – a real statesman. Tragically, he was killed in a truck bomb outside his offices just weeks later. It came at a huge detriment to the international effort as the UN left the country. We were sure that it was an inside job, ordered by the Iraqi opposition.

Working with Jerry Bremer was difficult; his headquarters was never fully populated and it was hard to find the right people. We were lucky to have Bernard Kerik, a former chief of New York Police during 9/11, and Deputy Chief Constable Doug Brand, who joined us from the Yorkshire police force to work with Bernie. Getting the right level of support for Doug was very frustrating and needed repeated requests to deploy the right staff, armoured cars and protection teams so that he could operate independently. Getting the right reaction from the Foreign Office felt rather like punching into cotton wool. It was as if, once Doug had been sent out, the FCO had solved the problem and it had gone away. Thanks to the help we had from the MOD Iraq planning team, we eventually got what we needed. Doug and I have kept in touch. Fortunately, those in Jerry's inner cohort were good allies so we soon had a team of experts ready to begin to help get the country on its feet again – power, oil, transport, security. Walt Slocombe, a key advisor during Bill Clinton's Presidency, and, later, Andy Bearpark, both proved to be energetic and straight-talking people and were good to have around.

Jerry Bremer, a man with a long history of nation-building, was impatient to see results and was not helped by the interference from George Bush's Defence Secretary, Donald Rumsfeld, who would pester him constantly with regular phone calls issuing more priorities, known as 'Snowflakes'. As the days passed, oil fires broke out, the fuel wasn't getting through to the pumps, and the population was growing impatient and began killing coalition forces. Smuggling was rife. The honeymoon was over and the US forces began to learn some hard lessons about counter-insurgency operations as the death toll continued to rise. I brought in a team of trainers to give the US troops some skills and tips about how to operate in a hostile, well-armed environment and Brigadier Brunt, still then in my old headquarters in Wilton, did a great job to fly out 1,000 personal role radios that would enable troops on patrol to talk to each other. The Americans weren't equipped to do that.

Despite the challenges and frustrations we faced, our daily briefings at 06:00 slowly began to see some limited signs of improvement and we got some results. Saddam's sons, Ouday and Qsai, were both on the wanted list and were discovered lying low in a house in Mosul. A fire fight ensued, the house was destroyed and Saddam's sons and two others were killed. News travels fast in Iraq and the celebratory fire could be heard when Jerry held his press conference to announce their deaths. Coalition Forces continued their efforts to capture other wanted characters, including Saddam Hussein, and the search for the illusive and much-vaunted weapons of mass destruction, while Marty Dempsey collected tonnes of unwanted weapons from Baghdad.

Truckloads were removed on a daily basis. Meanwhile, we kept taking casualties and I was glad to see the defences of Maude House improved and my four-tonne armoured Land Rovers appear. Working with Andy Bearpark, who was employed by the Foreign Office to take charge of Iraq's reconstruction effort (principally oil and electricity), and Colonel Mac McEwan, who worked in the American headquarters within Saddam's palace and was responsible for coordinating our logistical support functions (police, engineers, medical, legal), we also improved the 'machinery' to get the Coalition effort working more effectively; the exchange of the new Iraqi currency was the real benefit of that.

Returning to Baghdad in 2003 after Brendan's wedding (I made it, as ordered, and it was a wonderful day), our regular visitors from the UK and the US continued to be disappointed and frustrated at what they found in the country and were surprised at the lack of support coming from London. Despite claims to the contrary, the Government was no longer focussed on Iraq, and the Prime Minister's statement that the UK would rebuild the country on a 'war footing' was without foundation. Put simply, there was no plan and we were reacting to events, trying to limit the damage where we could. And it was hot: I recall one day the heat of 56°C at Baghdad airport. Even my bodyguard, Corporal Rob Bartrum, became a hospital case that day.

Maude House was a big place and offered plenty of scope to expand. Earlier in my time there, I had established links with Chris Sagar who was the UK's Ambassador in the British Embassy in Baghdad. The embassy had been evacuated in the 1970s and the staff had to leave in such a hurry that the office paperwork was in the filing cabinets and the official staff cars were still there in the garage, dusty but with the Ambassador's flag flying. The embassy and grounds (including a swimming pool) had been managed by a loyal Iraqi until the fall of the

Saddam regime. At that point, the Foreign Office deployed its new 'fly away' embassy, which was occupied by Chris and his team. The place was guarded by a small force provided by the UK division based in Basra. But it was still vulnerable to attack by hostile forces or, even worse, a truck bomb crashing through the gates. We needed an evacuation plan and made arrangements to bring the embassy staff back to Maude House (by river if necessary) if we received the agreed code word. We were confident that we could accommodate up to sixty people, if necessary, and still let the embassy staff function. At 04:00 one morning, the phone rang incessantly. I answered and the ambassador's deputy issued the code.

Intelligence had been received of an impending assault on the embassy and they wanted to evacuate, immediately. I agreed, woke the team and asked for a brew as we awaited their arrival. As the first elements of the staff arrived, I was advised to evacuate the whole team straight away as it was too dangerous to stay. I thought that this was a bit too dramatic; this was British Territory and we weren't facing thousands of Mexicans at The Alamo yet. A withdrawal now by the British on the basis of one unconfirmed report would do untold damage to our national reputation. It's just not British to do that. I rang the guard commander and he reassured me that it was very quiet, the locals were still friendly – nothing to worry about.

"Do you want to come back?" I asked him.

"Out of the f'ing question", he said. "If we leave now it would be a nightmare to get back in to the embassy again. If we left, the locals would be in and steal most of it if we don't protect the place. We're staying."

I agreed and told the MOD. Thankfully, the drama ended with no attack and the staff returned to a secure site a few days later. The guard did a good job and we proved the evacuation plan worked – apart from the river boat ride.

Soon, the time came for me to leave Iraq and get ready for my next post: Military Secretary based at the Army Personnel Centre in Glasgow. My replacement was General Andrew Figgures (whose surname confused the Americans when I introduced them – they probably thought we were related!) and, after a most enjoyable farewell dinner hosted by Ric Sanchez with his staff present, I made my way home, disappointed that we could and should have done more.

But I wasn't finished with Iraq just yet.

I became the Military Secretary in 2003 and, in the next year, I was tasked by the MOD to go to Washington to appear before the House Armed Forces Committee and give evidence on the ongoing stability operations in Iraq. I was to appear with my Australian and Polish counterparts as all of us had troops there from the outset. Fortunately, my good friend from our days in Bramcote, Brigadier John Keeling, was serving at the US embassy as the military attache and he kindly offered to put me up in their home and take me to Capitol Hill for the hearing. The session itself was conducted in a very friendly atmosphere and I was able to handle the questions from Congress about progress quite easily. The session was broadcast live and in front of a sizeable, interested audience. The panel was friendly and at pains to ask us to thank our Governments for the work that the military was doing and to continue our commitment to the operation. We promised to do that.

Staying at John's house in May marked another remarkable event – and a national occasion – as thousands of cicada bugs emerged from their burrows. These bugs grow under deciduous trees and live for just a few weeks. Eggs are laid in the burrows and the bugs do not emerge again for another 17 years. My visit happened to coincide with the cicada invasion and, as I went outside for a smoke break, I could hear the buzzing and was dive bombed as these bugs crashed landed on and around me. I survived the onslaught and, shortly after my trip, the bugs died, not to appear again for another 17 years. It was a memorable way to finish my US visit.

In 2009, the then Prime Minister, Gordon Brown, announced that there was to be an inquiry led by Sir John Chilcott, with my old boss from the MOD, Margaret Aldred, acting as his Secretariat. Together with Andrew Figgures, I was called to give evidence to the inquiry.

The inquiry report was published in 2017, some eight years after it started. Sir John Chilcott received a lot of criticism for the time he had taken since he started his work but that is perfectly understandable given the requirements laid on him by the Government – the terms of reference he was given left him no option. The families affected by the deaths and injuries of the soldiers in that campaign were understandably frustrated by the delay but, in my view, it is far better to take however long needed to get the facts right than to resist the temptation to publish early and be found wanting later on. The report when it was published was comprehensive and detailed and the summary by the Chairman was brutally frank and honest. There are no winners in a campaign of this nature and the effects of our engagement here are still being seen across the region and the wider world. That will continue for many years and we in this country are not alone in facing them.

I think Sir John's inquiry report was an excellent piece of work and I agree with his summary – with one exception. Sir John did not believe that the Prime Minister set out to persuade Parliament to send troops to Iraq. I think that, having determined to support President Bush, the PM set out to deliver whatever he had to do and gained the Government's to support to do it.

I admire Tony Blair but, on this occasion, he got it wrong.

There are a number of lessons to identify after Iraq that are not worth repeating here. The evidence I gave to John Chilcot can be found on the Web at Iraqinquiry.org.uk. The notes given to the inquiry appear in the appendix of this book and expand on that.

MILITARY SECRETARY & ADJUTANT GENERAL

In 2005, I became Adjutant General.

I had had an excellent grounding; my previous posting in Glasgow as the Military Secretary, or MS, was a role all about people. As MS, I was responsible for looking after the whole Army including its regular and reserve components and getting them posted to the right place at the right time so that they were capable of doing what the country required of them. The Army was facing a complex mix of challenges: we had been going through a series of reductions; recruitment was poor and we were losing too many people; retention was a key concern and we were struggling to meet the demands of the growing number of overseas operational tour plots without breaking the laid-down policy of tour intervals (two years' break before being deployed again).

My teams represented all the Regiments and units of the Army, professional and territorial alike, with a broad range of trades, skills and expertise. Men and women and the contingent of soldiers from overseas and the Commonwealth countries required their own particular treatment to ensure that their cultural and traditional expectations were met. It was a good structure with well-known processes for people management and it left me to concentrate on perhaps the most challenging aspect: looking after the senior officer command plot – colonels, brigadiers and generals – and ensuring that I was placing the right individuals in to the right posts, suitably qualified and experienced to do the job.

Once again, there was a well-known and practised system for doing this; interviews were held, gradings for promotion and appointment boards were programmed and, after a series of visits to the senior commanders to obtain their views, formal meetings agreed the proposed plans and the results were promulgated. It was important for me to be trusted, discreet and approachable in the eyes of the individuals concerned, a number of whom were rather more ambitious than was reasonable to expect: the Army had reduced in strength and it was clear that not all of them could ever reach the lofty heights of Head of the Army. By far the majority were good men and women and were realistic about their potential but others took some persuading. Being honest wasn't always easy but those affected generally took disappointing news well. Thankfully, I was trusted to look after my people properly and I tried hard to do that. I was helped in this by travelling around the Army to meet the officers and tell them what was happening.

Visits to the UK, Germany and the USA, where we had a significant presence, were particularly enjoyable and allowed me to test the views of those in the audience and report back when I needed to. My visits called for a good deal of flying and I spent a number of hours on a train, in the car or in the waiting rooms of Glasgow airport; six airports in one week was my record but with some careful planning, I was able to spend most weekends at home.

In time, I began to think about my next post. My own personal gradings of potential for promotion were good. There was only one job that really interested me, that of Adjutant General (AG). My predecessor was about to retire and I knew that I could do the job; my work on the Human Resources Strategy in the 1990s had given me further good grounding in people issues and I would get one last chance to work with Jacko as Chief of General Staff (CGS), again, before his possible retirement. I entered my name into the running and, eventually, the appointments board met to discuss the post. As Chairman of the Board, CGS sent me out of the room ("so that we can talk about you."). I left and, knowing that I had the support of some members, felt pretty confident. Time went on and I began to get a bit concerned; *it's not a given*, I thought. Eventually, I was called back in: "You're to be AG, Freddie," Jacko said. "Well done. Next item."

As I continued as MS, one of my duties was to be part of the Honours and Awards Committee. Here, we assessed those who had been recommended for Honours and Gallantry Awards. Honours, typically orders of the Bath and British Empire, marked an individual's performance at a specific duty or cause and recognised service given. Following a review by Sir Michael Quinlan, the amount of awards we could recommend were strictly controlled. The quotas he laid down had to be met and there were far too many candidates who really deserved to be awarded but whom we could not accept. The committee worked to a numbers system where citations were graded: one for unlikely to ten for outstanding. We rarely differed in the awards we gave, so discussion was usually straightforward and our recommendations went on to the Army Board for approval.

Gallantry awards were a different matter. Operations in Iraq and Afghanistan produced a large number of citations to consider. Such was the bravery, dedication and courage shown by our men and women that they would have made fine material for a movie. Again, we used the numerical grading system to prioritise the recommended list and, on one occasion, we read of an individual being recommended for a Conspicuous Gallantry Cross. We all graded him ten and were about to move on when a Committee Member said: "We've all given him ten. What else did he need to do to be awarded the VC?" We looked again at the citation and decided that he did everything expected of him and more. We agreed to submit the recommendation but this time for the award of a Victoria Cross.

The process takes time to complete and eventually goes to the sovereign for approval. When I got the news I had become AG, I was delighted to learn that Lance Corporal Johnson Gideon Beharry was indeed to receive the Victoria Cross. There then followed a rush of media interest at home, in Europe and his home of Grenada. Johnson was much in demand and there was talk of a book, painting and film. Army units wanted to see him and hear his story. Johnson was still an injured man and recovering, so I arranged a meeting with the head of the VC Association and agreed to act as his mentor. I would take demands for his time and talk to him to see if he wanted to do it. He was usually very cooperative but sometimes needed a little encouragement. All in all, and with direction, a thoroughly good soldier.

As AG, I was once asked if we should promote Johnson Beharry to Corporal by his parent unit. We sought authority but were told that, since his records showed that he had not completed the mandatory leadership course, promotion was not possible. I was amazed and frustrated. Without the exercise of a little common sense, it made the process a farce. I rang their office.

"Does a VC award count as a leadership course?" I asked

Silence, then sensing I was a little annoyed. "Yes, AG. It does. Promotion to Corporal agreed."

I kept in touch with Johnson Beharry until my stroke but I was delighted to see him at the Remembrance Parade in 2017 as a Lance Sergeant, wheeling Chelsea Pensioner the late Bill Speakman VC past the Cenotaph.

I was thrilled, if a bit daunted, to become AG, knowing that I was in for three hard years before I left the Army. I would have responsibility for all people issues and would be supported by the Heads of the Army's Training, Medical, Legal, Police, Education and Chaplaincy organisations. They were experts in their own fields. Being promoted to Lieutenant General and a seat on the Army Board was a bonus of course but, for me, it was the job that was the most important thing. I had three years to make a difference and fight for our soldiers and their families. I was retiring and did not have the ability or inclination to be CGS or work in the MOD again, so could say what I wanted. What could the system do? Hang me? Shoot me? Unlikely. This was my last shot and I wasn't going to lose the opportunity.

I arrived to find a lot going on in the people world. We were struggling to recruit the right numbers of young soldiers and were losing too many too early. A review into the much-reported Deepcut saga, where four young soldiers died between 1995 and 2002, was underway and an eminent lawyer, Nicholas Blake QC, was to report his findings shortly. The Army's reputation as a caring, professional employer was being called into question. Blake's findings and recommendations – and our reaction to them – could have a fundamental impact on the wishes of parents and guardians to see their teenagers join up. It caused us to change the way we recruited, organised and trained our young soldiers to prevent it from happening again.

One of the causes of the Deepcut tragedy was the weakness in supervision arrangements. Training at Deepcut was delivered by contract instructors who were mainly civilians. They appeared at about 08:00 to begin teaching and were generally gone by

16:00. From then on, the recruits were left to their own devices, largely unsupervised. One or two non-commissioned officers were left to look after fifty or so young recruits, boys and girls. I recalled my time at Bramcote in the 1970s, when I had three NCOs looking after the same number of men. The scope for bad behaviour by hot-blooded youngsters was real, so leaving them unsupervised and under-occupied from dusk till dawn was a clear risk. The Army was still undermanned, hollowed out in its rank structure while its units treated manning the training organisation as a low priority. It was perhaps inevitable that the system led to the Deepcut scenario.

I felt that while I could not do much now about Deepcut, I could change the way training was approached and governed. We restructured the training organisation to ensure that the young recruits, aged sixteen, assembled in one college (The Army Foundation College, Harrogate), leaving the older ones to undergo the first phase of basic training at Pirbright, Winchester, Catterick and Edinburgh, before going on to their parent Regiments. It proved a much better approach and gave the young ones more time to grow up.

With some surprising reluctance from the commander, I directed that each training Regiment in the UK must create an Army Recruit Advisory Board. Made up of civilians and experts in the recruiting and training environment, including instruction and accreditation, medical, physiotherapy, discipline, health and hygiene, I asked the Board to submit a six-monthly report on the issues facing the Regiment. This was akin to the PTA, the Parent Teachers Association, and I encouraged the Board to conduct no-notice inspections with a free rein to go anywhere and speak to any young recruit about what he or she was up to. It took a little while to get going but, eventually, these reports started to gain traction and produce some very good recommendations.

Then, having established a school at Pirbright, I directed

that at any instructor appointed to the training Regiment had to attend an induction course and be taught the characteristics of the recruits joining the Army. It was a mandatory course where attendance was recorded by the Posting Authority and ensured that the instructor was well briefed before meeting the recruit for the first time. I visited the school from time to time and it was well received.

I have no idea if the Board and school have continued in the years since, but I hope they have done. I'm sure that, even if supervisory rates haven't improved, these arrangements will have gone a long way to avoiding another Deepcut.

It became clear soon after my arrival that our military criminal justice system was way under par. The time taken to process an offence and, if necessary, bring it before a court was taking too long. We had to deal with these allegations without fear or favour but, for a variety of reasons, the different agencies were just too slow. 'Justice delayed is justice denied' is often quoted and I sensed that we were vulnerable here, as we were when it came to investigating claims of wrong or inappropriate behaviour, on which the Army Board was asked to give its judgement. Part of the problem was that a number of those in the military chain of command did not really understand how the Army's legal system worked; as AG, I was responsible for disciplinary issues and I was supported by a senior lawyer, Major General David Howells. David looked after the careers of our professional lawyers and he also held the post of Army Prosecuting Authority. He could give advice on legal matters but was independent in his decision making. This was to present some very difficult decisions for us and we had to get it right. We were always conscious that to get a disciplinary case wrong might lead to an appeal to the Army Board or a Judicial Review. A bad decision would have a detrimental effect on the Army as a responsible, caring employer. We dealt with several cases involving theft and violence. David was an exceptional lawyer and I trusted his advice completely. I established the Delay Action Group and that went some way to improving matters.

In my first year, I also had another tricky matter to deal with; I was required to combine two senior Army headquarters (that of the Commander in Chief in Wilton and my own in Upavon) and relocate them, while reducing staff, improving working practices and doing it all at a reasonable cost. The idea was called Project Hyperion and it sounded pretty easy at first sight – put A and B together, move it to C and do it all for D – but things had changed. Now, the bureaucrats in the MOD were deeply into process and wanted to see our work at the important stages. We had a management structure to oversee and approve each stage. Staff officers in the two headquarters and the MOD felt that they had the right answer. As the head of the project team, I had served in both headquarters and in the ministry, so understood how business was done but we went through the motions, knowing that the answer was indeed simple. Andover in Hampshire was the only suitable and logical place for the relocated headquarters but we had to examine all the options before we decided that, actually, Andover was indeed right. It was already a functioning headquarters, originally a Royal Air Force Station, with plenty of scope for expansion and well-established communication links (A303/M3, Southampton airport, trains to London, helicopter landing sites). It could deal with our needs at minimal additional cost and was the obvious choice for the combined headquarters. Others, trying to be helpful, suggested a brand new build at Solstice Park near Amesbury (daft) or somewhere on Salisbury Plain Training Area (even more so), which was prohibitively expensive and couldn't be achieved in the time allowed. It hadn't been thought through at all. Mercifully, we moved on. Playing this game until we came up with the agreed and funded plan was the least enjoyable part of my role. Learning to bite my lip and deal with the frustration of delay and obfuscation when we knew that it could be done more quickly and save money became a useful skill. Three years after we started this exercise, we came up with the solution and began the move to Andover. We could have saved a lot of time, trouble and cost.

In 2006, as General Sir Richard Dannatt replaced Sir Mike Jackson as CGS, I was wrestling with a further frustrating issue. As part of the Army's ongoing plan to restructure the Infantry, the Royal Irish Rangers were to become The Royal Irish and combine their regular soldiers and the reserve into a more cohesive force. The plan entailed the disbandment of the Ulster Defence Regiment, the UDR. After around fifty years in existence, with so many murdered by the IRA in the Troubles, there was a clear need to recognise their last day of Service properly. Time passed and the final parade was approaching fast. My efforts to get positive support from the MOD was met with a lukewarm response in the extreme and my proposals to change the Regiment's title or adjust its flag by including a battle honour were rejected. Richard wanted a solution. I then spoke to a senior officer, who had served with the Irish Rangers, who said that whatever we did would be fine by him. Very helpful. Sensing that no-one was interested or wanted to do anything that might upset the Northern Ireland Peace Process, I was getting nowhere, so I decided that I had to break the logjam. I spoke to another retired Ranger, who knew more about Irish political-military matters and sensitivities than I ever would on my phone at home for about an hour and examined the various options open to us. The plan we agreed was to follow the Malta model. Malta was awarded the George Cross to mark the bombing and suffering caused by the Germans during WW2 and we felt that the award of a Conspicuous Gallantry Cross (the second highest award) for the UDR would be appropriate. I thanked him and said I would go ahead.

Knowing that time was very short and that any approach to the MOD would be likely to fail, I asked our expert, Brigadier Jamie Gordon, to prepare the brief and CGC citation. His work was typically persuasive, quick and impressive. Knowing that the Queen would have to approve the honour, I contacted Her Private Secretary direct and explained my problem. He got the point immediately and asked to see the brief. We sent it up and he returned my call within the hour.

"I've shown the brief to Her Majesty," he said. "She has approved your recommendation. CGC it is."

Brilliant! If the Queen so directs, then we're there. Stuff the process and pinhead dancing – not even the MOD can oppose that. I gave Jamie the green light and, just days later, the Queen, accompanied by the Duke of York, Honorary Colonel of the Royal Irish, and by Adam Ingram MP, Minister for the Armed Forces in the MOD, presented the CGC to the Parade Commander. It was a good day. I heard nothing more from the MOD but was to see The Duke of York later and he told me that the Royal Irish/UDR ceremony had gone well.

One of my other tasks as AG was to invite selected guests to dinner to explain what was going on in the Army and perhaps deal with the often misreported stories about us. It was a major element of the information campaign and we met many interesting guests, including Bob Ainsworth the Defence Secretary, Sir Max Hastings, Kate Adie, Lords Bramall and Guthrie and the SAS command team. Wanting to thank Bob Rogers, the President of the Rugby Football Union, for the use of Twickenham for the annual Army vs Navy game, we invited Bob and his wife Janet to dinner. Jane and Sarah Jane Shirreff were seated next to Bob, and they told him about how we were treating the soldiers, who were returning badly-wounded from Iraq and Afghanistan at Selly Oak and Hedley Court. Sarah Jane told him all about the rapidly growing Help for Heroes initiative and the benefits that were planned for it at Hedley Court as more and more people were donating funds.

Bob was clearly interested to hear this, took it all in and said little about it. Later, we heard that, as President and on behalf of the RFU, Bob invited wounded warriors and escorts from Hedley Court to visit an international match at Twickenham as guests. A party of about ten accepted and went to the game, were featured in the match programme, introduced and given a standing ovation by about 90,000 fans. This was a tremendous gesture and we got to know Bob and Janet well over the years. We often meet at Twickenham to enjoy the Six Nations tournaments. They are very generous people.

Among all the other usual daily things going on, various matters and challenges are seared in my memory.

Our preparation to deploy on operations overseas needed close attention to ensure that our training was sufficient, support was adequate and our men and women were appropriately supported in coming to terms with the sometimes dangerous and demanding situations they endured. Medical support needed addressing: we had to ensure that we were looking after the families of those who had been killed and providing meaningful support to the seriously injured.

Medically, we were suffering a number of serious casualties in Iraq and Afghanistan, primarily gunshot wounds and soldiers losing limbs following roadside bombs. The UK's primary treatment centre for the wounded was Selly Oak Hospital in Birmingham. We were not ready to deal with the numbers coming through, give them the treatment they needed and get them on the road to recovery. The hospital staff did their best but could not deal with a soldier coming home, often in a coma, whilst getting the management of his or her care right. Selly Oak was essentially an old building and a training base for nurses (civilian and military) and it was unprepared to receive and treat the casualties we were receiving from Iraq. The treatment process could not handle the stresses (real and psychological) of soldiers being evacuated with missing limbs.

Injured military personnel were placed in mixed wards, suffering flashbacks and nightmares; metal bin lids that crashed when closed and sounded like explosions were frightening. The nurses witnessed some pretty unpleasant sights as they treated wounds safely and tried to prevent poison and contamination. The welfare facilities for the injured were also inadequate (too few allowances, inadequate longer-term planning after recovery, and the inability to make telephone calls) and there was no provision to accommodate the families who were visiting the wounded, often for a number of days and weeks and from long distances. In short, and despite the best efforts of the Chief Executive, Selly Oak was clearly not fit for purpose in the early days and our soldiers knew it. They did not want to end up there.

One casualty I saw on my visit made a big impression on me; Sergeant Andy Newell, a Pathfinder of the Parachute Regiment, was dealing with a complicated gunshot wound. The look he gave me from his hospital bed left me in no doubt that things had to change. He was telling me to get it sorted and I told him I would. We were failing our soldiers and it made me angry. At least I could give him a packet of fags as a friendly gesture. We stayed in touch after his release. A great soldier.

We needed a step change. My post-visit report to the Secretary of State was damning and it got some reaction but change didn't really start until we put a senior, experienced doctor into the place. Colonel Chris Parker created a care pathway and his presence made a real difference. Facilities for the families were enhanced and we began to improve the allowance package for the injured. Selly Oak owes Chris and everyone else involved in this important work a great deal and, now relocated to a new building, the hospital is much more what it should have been in the first place.

Ben Parkinson, a big, fit paratrooper, was another injured soldier to leave an impression. Ben was very badly injured by a roadside bomb in Afghanistan, which blew him clear of his vehicle. He lost both his legs, injured his spleen and his brain was severely affected. It was only luck and the sheer guts and determination of both Ben and his mother, Diane, as she cared for him in hospital, which saved him. I visited them in Putney hospital. She was very worried about what the future held, particularly the financial support she would get for his long-term recovery. Ben was going to recover, of that she was in no doubt but it would take years and she could get no sense out of the MOD. With tears in her tired eyes, she looked straight at me and said, "Don't make me beg." I promised her I would do what I could.

The first avenue we explored was the compensation scheme being offered by the MOD. The formula was bewildering. It was impossible to follow the logic of what Ben would receive and the amount offered was derisory; it was quite clear that Ben was going to need a custom built bungalow, designed to support a man living permanently in a wheelchair so that he could eat, sleep and keep himself clean every day, as well as have enough money to live on a daily basis. We got no sense of support from those responsible, so I decided to elevate the issue and invited Mr Derek Twigg, a Minister in the MOD, to visit Ben and see why I was making such a fuss. He agreed and I accompanied him to Putney, where I was met by his host (the hospital Chief Executive) and proceeded to listen impatiently to a fruitless, frustrating briefing about what Putney did. As we finished, Twigg's private secretary suggested that time had moved on and they ought to leave. I was furious and said that Ben was upstairs and had been waiting for us; we should go there straight away. We went and met Ben's family.

Ben was not a pretty sight and was unaware of what was happening. Calmly, Diane explained what was going on with his progress and what she expected. It was clear the Minister had got the message and he raised it with his staff when he got back. Typically, there was resistance to making any big change (one civil servant advisor even cautioned his boss to beware the 'pain of affordability') but, eventually, Ben received a significant increase in his compensation award. It was certainly a step in the right direction but it wasn't until a review was conducted by Lord Boyce, a former Chief of the Defence Staff, that common sense prevailed and the system was tightened up. I felt proud that we had achieved a good outcome but thought that we should never have got to that stage in the first place. Ben has since gone on to make remarkable progress. His mother Diane deserves huge credit for that.

Over the Christmas and New Year break of 2007, I took a call from Jacko. He told me that the media had got hold of news, photographs and interviews about the very poor condition of Army housing, was going to run a story and wanted to interview him. What did I think? I said that, because this was my area and I was aware of the facts (the story was accurate, quarters were very unsatisfactory and suffered from under-investment), he should let me do the interview instead. I felt that this was likely to be a major story and would give the media the opportunity to criticise the Army. In preparing my lines, I knew that I had three audiences to satisfy: the MOD, the media and the families living in these unsatisfactory houses. The families, particularly, needed to know that I understood the problem and was on their side. As the interview progressed, I said that the Military Covenant (something we stressed as part of the Army's Human Resources Strategy) was out of balance and we needed more resources to put it right.

The story was covered extensively on TV and radio over the

ensuing days. In follow up interviews, I argued for decency in whatever we did: decent training, decent pay, decent housing, decent equipment and so on. This did not go down very well; a Labour MP and member of the All Party Defence Committee alleged that I was making things up and I was grateful that Air Marshal Sir Jock Stirrup (the then Chief of Defence Staff) supported what I had said. Undeterred, the MP then proceeded to bombard my headquarters with a series of Parliamentary Questions about me and my lifestyle; the staff I employed, what I spent and where, and who I entertained in my quarter. His tactics were obvious: he was angry with what I had said and was going after me. Soon, the inevitable happened and my lifestyle was exposed in the Sunday papers, claiming that I was living like a lord while my soldiers lived in squalor. Knowing that my expenses were justified and that I was not being held responsible for the state of Army housing, I was determined to get an apology from the papers, for Jane's sake as much as my own. My own advisers told me not to bother – it was a story that had gone away and no-one was that fussed about it anyway. I disagreed; it was untrue and I couldn't ignore it. Whoever leaked the story had to realise that I would fight back. Eventually, and after weeks of asking, the civil servants gave me what I wanted, a simple statement that I was not responsible for Army housing and was not being blamed for its condition. The papers got that and apologised (albeit by writing a tiny statement, tucked away on the inside pages). I was satisfied, although, as I write this, I have received no apology from the Labour MP.

As my struggle with the media continued, another story was breaking; in Iraq a hotel worker called Baha Mousa was arrested and taken back to the base occupied by the Queen's Lancashire Regiment. Some hours later, he died in custody. The post mortem showed that he had over ninety injuries inflicted on his body. An ensuing investigation showed that Mousa had been treated in contravention of the Geneva Convention, tortured, and eventually died of his wounds. The photographs were sickening and, after detailed investigations, charges amounting to war crimes were laid against the Commanding Officer and six others. This was a difficult time for the Army and its reputation on operations; it needed some careful handling and I wished I had followed my instinct and not taken the advice of those around me. We were required to investigate these incidents without fear or favour but always on the basis of a principle that we assume innocence before guilt. This caused some difficulty and the advice I was getting from the staff on one particular issue about career management made me extremely nervous. Reluctantly, I was persuaded to follow the advice given to me and I submitted a briefing note to key members of the Army Board to seek their agreement. They refused because we were not following the principle demanded of us. They were right to do so and this made me angry and embarrassed that I had not followed my instinct and driven the decision to the right outcome. Fortunately, no damage was done and the court martial went ahead. It found no case against six and one other, Corporal Paine, was sentenced for inhumane treatment. Later, Baha Mousa's family was flown from Iraq to the UK and a compensation deal of several millions of pounds was agreed.

As we entered 2008, my mind turned towards retirement, although there was plenty left to do before I was finished, particularly in relation to the Military Covenant and securing decent conditions for soldiers.

I had not thought about my next step at all until I attended a memorial service to commemorate the losses in Bosnia at the National Arboretum in Litchfield. Among the guests was General Sir Mike Willcocks. He had been my boss during my tour there in 1999 and, after retirement from Service, took up the post of Black Rod in the House of Lords. He told me that he was retiring the following year and had I thought about what I would do next? I said that I had not but, because he thought I could do the Black Rod job, he invited me to lunch anyway to talk about it. I went, Mike told me what was involved and urged me to apply. I realised that this was something I could do.

As I was leaving the Army, I submitted a proposal to better support our veterans in need. I was exposed to something of this in my job and could see that all the various charitable organisations involved were in need of better coordination so that the focus was where it needed to be. I proposed the creation of a Veterans Commissioner to provide the function with a small team. The idea was supported by several experienced senior officers, including Jacko, Richard Dannatt and David Richards. Ministers in the MOD liked the idea but some civilian advisors and other senior military officers didn't back it. When I left, I received a charming letter from the Secretary of State, thanking me for what I had done. I took the liberty of sending him a copy of my proposal about the commissioner. Eventually, I got a reply from the Labour MP Kevan Jones telling me that, as there was no evidence of the need, he would not support it. I knew he was wrong – there was plenty of evidence – but I left it there.

It was a shame – the case for is still strong; in 2017 the Charities Commission reported that there were 187 charities registered with their organisation. A significant proportion of that number will have a veteran focus and Michael Hockney, who conducted a major review of the issues facing veterans, recommended among other things the creation of a commissioner. I wish Mr Jones had listened to his advisors.

As my retirement was approaching, I was invited to Hereford to say farewell to the Special Air Service. I had seen a great deal of the Regiment over the years and seen them in operations in the UK, the Balkans and Middle East. I had attended their boxing charity nights and supported the CO at funerals when one of their own had been killed in action. I saw that we had been placing extraordinary demands on the Troopers' commitment on six-month operational tours, day after day and often well into the night, when lives were at risk. Absence away from home on operational duty was becoming an issue for retention and I was determined to do more to recognise what we were asking of them. I was delighted when the Armed Forces Pay Review Body recommended a significant sum in recognition of their contribution. I hope it worked.

Jane received a phone call from the SAS just before my visit and was asked if it was all right if they took me for a tandem parachute jump. She said it would be fine – just don't break him. The day arrived, I flew to meet the CO and his RSM to be told that parachuting was off as the weather was too poor, so I was taken off to do some anti-ambush drills with my close protection team and shooting practice. Following a good lunch, we moved off to the Sergeant's Mess where I was presented with a bottle of Famous Grouse whisky with the famous Hereford cap badge and an engraved golf putter, thanking me for my support. I found it difficult to find the words to thank them but did say that I would think of them every time I missed a short putt on the course. I still do and I am proud to have known them and the jobs they have done on our behalf.

I left the Adjutant General post having had great support and advice from my staff, particularly my Military Assistants Greville, Andrew, Jim and Huw. The MAs kept me up to date with events going on in the wider Army and were excellent at keeping the papers flowing and judging the temperature and mood in the MOD. They had all commanded their own Infantry Battalions, often at the rough end of the operational spectrum and had to deal with some fairly stressful events including death, serious injury and bad discipline. They had an instinctive feel for what mattered and gave me come very good and wise advice on complicated issues. Someone I had known for many years, Sir Graeme Lamb, once described this to me as "Doing the right thing on a difficult day". He was right. Equally, my ADCs, Simon, Jonno and the brilliant Rachel, did me proud and kept my programme on track. Their ability to keep the plates spinning and a sense of humour were invaluable. In the office sat my PA, Wendy, a complete expert on IT systems and able to produce the paperwork instantly as and when I asked for it. We were delighted when she was awarded the MBE on the day she produced twin girls. I was pleased to call and give her the good news as she had been so busy she hadn't noticed it! I missed all these good people and would think of them often.

Jane gave me a wonderful surprise retirement party when lots of my friends turned up to celebrate. I realised that I was tired and needed a break so I relaxed as best I could – not an easy thing for me to do. I played good golf with some old friends and began to lose some weight but, soon enough, the time came to submit my application and CV to become Black Rod. I decided to give it a good go and, with Kate's help as scribe and proofreader, wrote the application papers and sent them in.

I was called to Westminster for interview and invited to give a five minute brief on a security matter. It showed that security was a big issue for Parliament and I talked about my role in the events after the Brighton bomb, supporting the police for the Conservative Conference in 1988. I don't know how many candidates were running for the post but I was selected for a second interview inside the House of Lords. My knowledge of the Lords' geography was pretty weak then but, fortunately, I had known Sir Gerald Howarth for some time. Gerald was the MP for Aldershot so we had a lot of military things in common and met quite frequently at various events. He offered to show me around and take me to the interview room.

Meeting for coffee in Portcullis House, we did the tour. My head was spinning as Gerald pointed out the important things of note. His knowledge was comprehensive and I realised that it would take some time for me to get to know the place, if I got the job. Gerald left me outside the Lord Speaker's office and I was called in by my prospective boss, Baroness Helene Hayman, alongside her deputy, the man who could be my immediate boss, Michael Pownall (entitled the Clerk of the Parliaments), and the Leaders of the Political Parties. Helene introduced me to them and asked a couple of questions before giving the other peers the chance to ask their own. It was a very informal, friendly session that I thoroughly enjoyed and felt that I had had a good interview. I left to go home and, a few days later, I was told that Her Majesty had approved the application. I was to become Black Rod in the spring of 2009.

My retirement from Service in 2008 was to be coloured by one significant disappointment. Shortly after I left the Army, the post of AG was removed, subsequently re-instated and, finally, the post was done away with completely and its responsibilities were divided up among other senior officers. I found this to be a great pity and a backward step. The voice and credibility of AG as the Army's personnel director had been removed and the media lost its chief spokesman when it wanted to explore a story about people issues. The nation had come to accept the concept and importance of the Military Covenant in looking after its soldiers and their families and the Government began to reflect the need for it in policy statements and election manifestos.

Removing the post of AG effectively buried the Covenant. The Army lost its lead voice and personnel champion. Regardless of the size of the Army, now and in the future, its soldiers and their families will always have difficult issues to be addressed. They can be complex and multi-faceted and will require a focal point to ensure that practical, balanced solutions can be reached.

If I had one wish, it would be to say to the Head of the Army: Re-establish the AG. Opportunities to achieve resilience and betterment are being missed and the Army is the loser.

My final tour as AG left me with several memorable moments including: being honoured with my knighthood in 2007, receiving so many letters of congratulation from my great friends and colleagues, and later being knighted by HRH the Prince of Wales; the Festival of Remembrance in the Albert Hall and ceremony in Westminster Abbey; attending various sporting events, particularly Wimbledon on men's semi-finals day and Twickenham for the annual Army vs Navy game. For Jane, she remembers especially being a guest to commemorate the Victoria Cross and George Cross Association with a service before Her Majesty in Westminster, where I watched Lance Corporal Johnson Gideon Beharry VC parade with the other VC/GC medal holders into the Abbey. I had been looking after Johnson's interests with the Head of the Association in the early stages of his injury, so it was a pleasure for me to see him on his feet.

These are memories that I will treasure.

BLACK ROD

Preparing to start my job as Black Rod in April 2009, I spent the months in between visiting Westminster and getting my uniform fitted. The black worn by officials in the Houses of Parliament signified that we had been in mourning on the orders of Queen Victoria to mark the death of Prince Albert in 1861 and remained so ever since. Tights were all the rage then too and I took some teasing about that. I watched and talked about the ceremonial aspects with my predecessor, Mike Willcocks, including the Mace procession during the opening of the Lords' Chamber, introducing new peers into the House and my main role in the State Opening of Parliament. I also met the team and knew that I would be well supported: Hedley Duncan, the Yeoman Usher, was my deputy and, while he was due to leave in the next few months, he was going to be a key player in coordinating our activities; Keith Phipps was the Principal Doorkeeper and, as an ex-Coldstream Guardsman, had seen and done it all. We talked the same language. His deputy, Dave Evans, was also a member of the Life Guards and a highly reliable stand-in should Keith be unavailable; and my wonderful staff who ran the front office for me: Jakki Perodeaux, Nicola Rivis and Jo Fuller, later Hendricks.

When the time came to take up my appointment, I reported

with Mike Willcocks to Buckingham Palace. We waited in the ante room until Mike was called in to see the Queen to say farewell. He re-appeared and it was my turn next. The Equerry showed me in, I bowed, said, "Your Majesty" and moved into the room where she was standing next to the Garter King of Arms. She shook my hand and Garter held up the Oath of Allegiance for me to read. She looked at me. Big moment! I read the Oath as I had heard so many times before without stumbling and at the end looked up at her and said, "Ma'am." She took the Rod from the Garter and handed it to me as she and other sovereigns would have done to my predecessors. "Well done. Black Rod – good luck." The job was mine and, at that point, theory crashed into reality. If things went wrong on my watch, it was my fault. Nothing like knowing that to focus the mind.

I soon adjusted to the rhythm of life there. The Palace of Westminster is probably the best known of all the places in the country and I took some time to get to know the layout of the buildings, its dark corridors and routes from the Lords to the Commons. Fortunately for me, the doorkeepers were ever helpful and would happily point me towards the committee rooms, refreshment facilities and the Lords' Terrace overlooking the Thames. This was a well-kept secret and one of the few places that I could sit over a coffee and smoke. It was also a very good source of gossip and intelligence as peers, like Lord Geddes and Baroness Faringdon, told me what was happening upstairs in the Chamber. I arranged quite a few meetings there and soon realised that their lordships, who were enjoying the same thing, were poorly supported. I set in train a project to provide them with what they needed: a telephone, TV screen showing the business of the day, and easier access for the staff. It made their lot and mine a little more comfortable.

My daily routine usually began before 8am, when I came to the House and used the quiet time to walk the corridors. This gave me a good feel that all was as it should be; the police and stewards were there, the cleaners were doing their stuff and the caterers were all present and ready to help. If there was a special occasion later in the day, particularly in the Lords Chamber, I would check that the right layout was there. Thereafter, I prepared for the programme of meetings with Michael Pownall the Clerk of the Parliaments and my boss, the Lord Speaker, the security staff, and, every Monday, with Keith Phipps, to talk through the forecast of events. Towards the afternoon, we got ready for the ceremony when the Chamber is opened for business: the Yeoman Usher carries the Mace and escorts the Lord Speaker to the Chamber. Wearing formal uniform of white tie, black tails and tights and carrying a sword, Black Rod joins the procession through the Peer's Lobby and into the Lords. Prayers, led by one of our bishops, is followed by thirty minutes of four questions and, at the end, the business of the day begins. I tended to leave soon after that for other commitments but was always available should I be needed in the office. I helped quite a few peers that way, dealing with Baroness Boothroyd's dodgy light bulb over her coat of arms, Lord Martin's office facilities and Lord Campbell of Alloway's missed lunch appointment with his daughter, to name but a few. Lord Campbell was famous for having escaped twice from Colditz as a Prisoner of War during WW2 and was very forgetful. His daughter was very understanding.

If the Yeoman Usher was otherwise occupied, my task in the evening was to be present when the House was closed ('adjourned'). This was difficult to guess but the Doorkeepers could usually give me a good estimate of when I might be needed. They understood the workings of the place better than I did and they had my number anyway. After adjournment, I usually got away at about 9pm and was back in my nearby flat by 9.30pm. The latest I ever had to stay was three in the morning – the Yeoman did well to miss that day!

About once a week, I was required to prepare new people to become a Baroness or a Lord and this was a particular pleasure for me. I met the person being introduced about a week beforehand, to talk them through the process, how I could help and show them a DVD of how it works. Once, while briefing Lord Sugar on his role, I pressed the start button on the DVD machine and nothing happened. I tried again and still nothing. *This is embarrassing*, I thought, *I'm sitting here with Lord Sugar, the founder of AMSTRAD and I can't even get the machine to work.* Fortunately, the third attempt was successful so my trial was over. I declined his offer to help, but I could see that Lord Sugar was amused too.

We would then walk through the ceremony and I would meet them on the day to conduct the ceremony itself. Baroness Kinnock, wife of Neil, was my first and was soon followed by a number of others. Lord Sugar, Baroness Tanni Grey Thompson (an outstanding athlete who gave the oath of allegiance in Welsh) and Lord Kakkar, who visited me in hospital, stay in my mind as particularly good and helpful people. The Bishops, Lords Freud and Coe were always friendly to me too.

Part of my role as a member of the Royal Household, and with the title of Officer of the Garter, was to take part in the Order of the Garter Ceremony. Each summer, the Queen and the holders of the Garter (one of the oldest orders of chivalry; there are only ever twenty-four members) assemble for lunch with the Queen in Windsor Castle and then process to St George's Chapel. Jane and I hired a driver for the journey from Westminster. A London lad, he had never been to Windsor before and his eyes were popping as he drove through the main arch into the castle; so much so that I had to warn him to watch where he was going or he would run over the young man dismounting from his motorcycle. It was Prince William, second in line to the throne. It would have made headline news if we had hit him

– and been the end of my job. Fortunately, HRH didn't notice the close shave and our driver stopped panicking. The royal procession and ceremony was done beautifully on a very hot day and represented all that was good about our country.

One of the most enjoyable aspects of the job was the opportunity to take friends and guests on a tour of the palace. It was a rare privilege to be able to do this as so few people had seen the layout and history and rarely appreciated what was televised during ceremonial occasions. I would follow the route taken during the State Opening of Parliament and let them see the Grand Staircase and the Robing Room, where the Queen enters to put on the Imperial State Crown, before processing into the Royal Gallery. The Royal Gallery is a beautiful space, surrounded by portraits of the royal family and dominated by two huge paintings by the prolific artist Daniel Maclise. Born in 1806, Maclise spent most of his working life in London and completed the Waterloo painting in 1859. It measures over thirteen metres wide and shows the Duke of Wellington, surrounded by the dead and wounded, meeting Field Marshal Blucher at La Belle Alliance. Blucher's arrival with his reserves was in the nick of time and turned the tide of the battle. On one occasion, I was asked by Field Marshal Lord Inge, a former Chief of Defence Staff to take a German party on the tour. Arriving at the gallery, I described the scene at Waterloo. As I was about to turn to move on, my German guest removed a business card from his wallet. His name was also Blucher and he told me he was a direct descendent of the famous man in the painting. It was an extraordinary coincidence, and I was glad that I knew a bit about the battle. Maclise's fabulous artwork is matched only by his other thirteen metre painting on the opposite side of the gallery, showing the death of Admiral Nelson at Trafalgar. Just as Terence Cuneo would conceal a mouse somewhere in his battle scenes, Maclise was believed to conceal a small cocktail glass in his. I only ever found three of them. They are not at all easy to spot.

Moving through the gallery into the Lords Chamber, I would show the guests the throne used by the Queen to deliver the speech before we then took the walk I followed between the Commons and the Lords. If the House was not in session – and with strict instructions not to take photographs – I would show them where I would knock on the door, the layout in the Commons, including the Speaker's Chair, the place for the Mace, despatch box, press gallery and front benches. Standing at the despatch box, I would remind people of the memorable and historic speeches that had been made from this spot by Prime Ministers and Leaders of the Loyal Opposition. It was certainly an interesting tour and I'm sure (hope!) our guests learned a lot from it. Our son, Brendan, certainly did and still remembers being given a tie to wear by Mr Phipps before entering the Lords Chamber to listen to the debate. Wise chap – he did as he was told.

Outside the palace were two other famous statues. Richard The Lionheart is mounted proudly guarding the Lords' car park while, just by the entrance to the House of Commons, Oliver Cromwell stands wearing his uniform from the Civil War as a stark reminder to Members. Oliver is looking downcast and it is easy to see why, for, directly opposite him on the wall of St Margaret's Church, is a tiny bust of King Charles's death mask. It is easy to understand the regret on Cromwell's face at having ordered his trial and execution.

By far my main and most important responsibility was to be the lead for my boss, the Lord Speaker Baroness Helene Hayman, on the security of the Palace of Westminster. It is a place known all over the world, a magnet for tourists and the Mother of all Parliaments. It was reported that something like a million people visited the palace every year and it was their right to do so, to see democracy in action and witness the proceedings in the House of Commons and in the Lords. These visits, however, had to be done in a controlled way; we were all familiar with and had seen the threat posed by terrorists and the impact of a spectacular attack on a world famous building of such import must be prevented. We simply had to keep it safe. The Metropolitan Police gave me a dedicated group of armed and unarmed police officers, we controlled access and movement safely with a critical eye and some sophisticated equipment, and our trained dogs searched the place regularly for explosives. Supported by an expert Parliamentary Security Coordinator, we held regular meetings on the security plan and what lay ahead. We felt secure enough but complacency was always the thing to beware of.

This was brought into sharp relief at the time of the Parliamentary Recess in the summer. As the House was about to return, I made a difficult phone call to the Lord Speaker to tell her that about forty people from Greenpeace had climbed onto the roof of Westminster Hall. The whole affair was filmed and it was a very well-planned and conducted, professional operation. The Greenpeace protestors said they would stay on the roof until Prime Minister Gordon Brown returned to the Commons. I had to tell some of the more angry Lords that I couldn't do what they thought I should do to get the protesters down. Eventually, the group gave up, were arrested, later to be charged and fined. Sadly, it hadn't rained so my prayers weren't answered.

The event showed that we could not relax. To learn some lessons, I arranged for a specialist Military Team to test our security systems. The team had done this before at many military bases and we gave them clear instructions about what was and was not allowed: no weapons, ID cards to be shown when asked, own up when challenged and only enact genuine attempts to breach our security plan. The exercise took place over the working week and only the Chief Superintendent responsible knew about it, so that he could get involved if necessary.

The team I used did well and, using some very basic skills, were able to breach the plan. I knew they had done it when I came into my office and found a calling card with the team commander's name on it. He left me a message on the reverse: "Sorry I missed you." My deputy did actually see him but he was on his way out by then. At the end of the exercise, the team produced a comprehensive report with photographic evidence to support what they had found and done to get in and the Superintendent was given a number of positive recommendations to follow up. It was a very successful exercise and I planned to do it again.

As well as my security duties, I also had some ceremonial functions to fulfil, including arranging visits by the Queen and by Heads of State to meet and speak to the Lords. Second to the State Opening of Parliament, Her Majesty's most important visit was to unveil her bust by the renowned sculptor, Oscar Nemon, whose other best known work is the statue of Winston Churchill in the House of Commons. The bust was very like the Queen's image on the postage stamp and remained unfinished after his death in 1985. The Queen came to see and unveil the bust in the Royal Gallery before it moved to its final place in the Robing Room. While planning for the visit, we decided to introduce to her a number of people who had been involved in preparing for the State Opening. We discovered that Oscar's daughter, Aurelia, was married to Sir George Young, who just happened to be my local MP. Meeting George and his family was a must and the Queen was delighted to make the connection, as she was to meet all those there who were involved in preparing for the State Opening, mostly from London and all with a great sense of cockney humour.

As the most important day in the Palace of Westminster's

calendar, the State Opening requires a great deal of preparation. It is the day when Her Majesty the Queen visits Westminster formally to open proceedings for the year and, reading the Queen's Speech from her throne in the House of Lords, tells the Lords and the MPs what her Government will do in the coming year. It is a major public occasion, televised extensively by the BBC, and it requires meticulous planning, rehearsal and preparation to present Westminster in the best possible light. The ceremony is steeped in history, dating from the Civil War, and it reflects the role of democratic government. The BBC has been covering the ceremony and knows the process backwards; a mistake here would be spotted immediately; we were on show and we had to get it right. The planning phase went on for weeks and, come the day, we were ready and wanted the whole thing go well. My job wouldn't last long if it didn't!

My role in the State Opening was largely ceremonial. As the Queen arrived and entered the Lords Chamber to her place on the throne, she signalled that she was ready to receive and address the Members of Parliament. Escorted by Mr Keith Phipps, my ever loyal Principal Doorkeeper and a police officer, I set off on the walk to the House of Commons door, which was slammed in my face as I arrived to commemorate an incident at the height of the Civil War when the King sent his guards to arrest a group of MPs.

Rehearsing this moment until we and the BBC were happy was vital – and the rehearsals taught us a few lessons. On one occasion the door was slammed a fraction too early and nearly took off the end of my nose. On another, Andy, my regular escort from the Metropolitan Police, was taken ill at the last minute and we needed a replacement. As I often said to my deputy – and was to be proved right on the day of my stroke, although I of course had no idea that I would be the one absent – we had to have a Plan B, in case a key player was unavailable. We searched for a stand-in policemen with a good, military-like bearing. We found one and he was clearly nervous about his role. As we carried out the dress rehearsal, I went through my routine in the Commons Chamber, knocked on the door and said my piece: "Mr Speaker, the Queen commands this Honourable House to attend Her Majesty immediately in the House of Peers."

We gathered afterwards and I said to Keith Phipps; "That seemed to go OK, Mr Phipps, but we must remember that the Queen doesn't like to be kept waiting. We need to step out."

He replied as only a Sandhurst trained guardsman instructor could do: "Correct Black Rod," and, turning to look at the police escort, said, "What Black Rod means, copper, is walk faster!"

Thankfully, the ceremony itself went well. We heard later that Her Majesty was happy. Mission accomplished.

The Lords made an indelible impression on me; I loved the job and I miss the place every day. There are too many Peers in the House and it causes undue strain on the management of the place. The time is right for change and, as I write this, it is encouraging to see that steps are underway to put the House on its right course. Since beginning this autobiography, I regret that, sadly, a number of Peers have died. I thank them all for the friendship and support they have shown to me and send their friends and families my condolences.

When May 2010 arrived, it was time to prepare for my second State Opening of Parliament. We began gearing up for the rehearsal.

Then, the stroke happened and my life changed forever.

Cypher: Third Regiment Royal Horse Artillery
(3RHA) Cypher

MOD (2): Day out with Directorate of Defence Policy. My boss,
Margaret Aldred, seated centre
London, March 1993

As Commander Royal Artillery, 3 UK Division, on my first tour of Bosnia, with my Command Team in the Tom Factory, Gornji Vakuf Bosnia, 1995

Guns firing at GLAMOC Ranges
Bosnia, 1995

A transporter delivering the vehicles into Bosnia – very cold and treacherous driving, average speed about 10k per hour
Bosnia 1995

Trying the local beverage, plum brandy, in the Sanski Most base. Awful
Bosnia 1995

Visit by Michael Portillo, then Secretary of State for Defence, talking to a soldier on observation duty. GLAMOC Ranges Bosnia 1995

Back in Bosnia for my second tour as Divisional Commander of Multinational Division South West, weapon training with the Czech battalion, Bosnia 1999

Visiting the Czechs in Kozarac with Gen Monty Meigs,
Commander Implementation Force,
Bosnia 1999

Barney, a weapons and explosives search dog, who later
came to live with us, much to Jane's annoyance
Bosnia, 1999

Visit by the Prime Minister, Tony Blair, en route to the International Summit in Sarajevo. I met him at Banja Luka airport and briefed him. He had no questions
Bosnia, 1999

In conversation with my 'interruptor' Elizabeta, meeting the Bosnia Commander in Sarajevo. My ADC Captain Richard Clements 2nd from left
Bosnia, 1999

With the Quartermaster 3RHA, Major 'Mac' Macpherson (centre) and Major Richard Nugee (left). Bosnia 1999

Handing over command to Major General Robin Brims. Bosnia had taken its toll – I look knackered! I was
Bosnia, 2000

General Sir Mike Jackson, Commander in Chief
Wilton, 2000

Left: Saddam's palace: HQ of the Coalition Provisional Authority (CPA) Baghdad, 2003

Below: With my team under the crossed swords in Baghdad. Saddam's hands were the models for holding the swords
Iraq, 2003

General Sir Mike Jackson GCB CBE DSO, Chief of the General Staff, visiting the Army Families Federation. WIth Sammie Crane, Chief Executive and me.
Upavon, Wiltshire 2006

State Opening of Parliament: On the Grand Staircase in the House of Lords awaiting the arrival of Her Majesty The Queen to be escorted by the Heralds. The Garter King of Arms is pictured in the front
Westminster, 2009

Lieutenant Colonel Sir Andrew Ford delivering the Imperial State Crown from the Tower of London into the Royal Gallery for the State Opening ceremony
Westminster, 2009

Waiting to set off for the Commons with Keith Phipps behind me and the Police escort behind him
Westminster, 2009

Knocking at the door of the Commons with the Rod, Westminster, 2009

Leading the Speaker, John Bercow, to the House of Lords Westminster, 2009

The Lord Great Chamberlain escorting Her Majesty The Queen to the carriage after the ceremony. She thanked me and the Earl Marshal [the Duke of Norfolk] (to my left) as she passed by. Westminster, 2009

THE ROAD BACK

MEDICAL JOURNEY

Excerpts from email updates sent by Jane to our friends and family, documenting the stroke, its immediate aftermath, and the long road to recovery... I have little or no knowledge of Jane's experience of events, so I am very grateful for her record of what happened.

First days:
I'm sorry to have to tell you that Freddie had a massive stroke on Tuesday morning (18 May 2010).

I arrived at the hospital at about 2pm and had a pretty depressing conversation with the doctor about quality of life decisions... and about two hours later, Freddie's condition started to deteriorate quite markedly. At that stage, the doctors asked me whether I would be willing for them to operate to remove a section of his skull; in someone of Freddie's age, the brain has not yet begun to shrink and consequently there was no room to allow the brain to swell – which it was certain to do, given the enormity of the stroke – without causing further, almost certainly fatal, damage. No choice really, so Freddie was transferred to the neurology department at King's College Hospital and the operation was carried out that night.

The following day, tests were carried out to determine the cause of the stroke, and it became apparent that it was a dissection of the aorta; there was a risk that it would rupture, which would definitely have been fatal, so once again Freddie was taken to surgery, for an operation that lasted six hours. As you know, Freddie is a real fighter – his last words to me before he went for his heart operation were 'we'll crack this' – it is going to be a long haul, though. It transpired that he had a genetic condition; as malformed aortic valve – it had only two sections, where a normal one has three – which had weakened over the years. Following this operation, Freddie suffered acute renal failure and massive bleeding, so had a further emergency operation in the early hours of the morning. He was transferred to the liver intensive care unit at King's, where he remained for a week, on dialysis and close monitoring. He was then moved to a High Dependency Cardiac Unit and, once the cardio-thoracic consultant was happy with his condition, returned to St Thomas's for rehabilitation.

Initial recovery:
The great news is that medically Freddie has made what I can only consider a miraculous recovery from the heart operations – the valve replacement and arterial repair are fine, the remaining kidney is doing its stuff, and blood tests show that the liver, despite giving a few ominous signals early on in the week, is now more or less doing what it should. No tubes anywhere now, which must be a huge relief to Freddie and he is out of hospital gowns... the wounds have healed really well, and he has been measured for a head cap (there is only skin between the outside world and his brain so protecting him from knocks and falls with a helmet is paramount). Once he has this, the physiotherapists

hope to get him into a 'tilt' wheelchair for a couple of hours each day, and are threatening him with the gym later this week… and I have been tasked with getting him some trainers and 'day clothes', which will give his morale a real boost.

Freddie's motor skills are great on the right side, and he is drinking and feeding himself and I am amazed at how much strength he still has (as were the physios, who unguardedly asked him to "hold tight") which means that he can pull himself up the bed, as well as into an upright position. There has been a marked improvement in the head swelling on his right side and he definitely has left side sensation and knows that it exists (apparently it can be quite common to 'ignore' a paralysed side) and I can occasionally feel resistance in his left leg, which is fantastically encouraging. He gets frustrated when asked to move it, though, and resorts to lifting the left leg with his right – he's very aware it's cheating, though, as he gives us a very knowing grin. He tires very easily and very suddenly and his body clock is pretty messed up – I don't think he has had a good night's sleep since the stroke, apart from when he was sedated, but I have been assured that this will sort itself out. He is quite disorientated still and tends to get anxious about meetings and rehearsals.

As for next steps – following initial assessments by consultant, physiotherapist, occupational therapist, speech and language therapists, a ninety-day rehabilitation plan will be put together. I have been told that this is going to be a long process, as full-on rehab can only start once the brain swelling has gone.

Milestones:
Freddie's sitting balance is great – he leans slightly to his left but that is mainly because of the loss of muscle tone that side. He is now getting himself off the bed and into a chair. In the gym he is doing standing 'leg push ups' and walking along a wall bar.

He has been out for trips round the hospital and grounds in a wheelchair, has visited the hospital cinema and had a haircut and a shower... his sense of humour is as bright as ever – on the day that he no longer needed the hoist, he told the physios he would rather miss the hookers! The temporary head cap has arrived and Freddie is able to put it on and off himself, and even do up the buckle one handed. It gives him (and me) a measure of confidence when he is being moved about.

The brain side of things is taking longer to improve. He still gets quite confused, particularly when he is tired. Things that we take so much for granted are obviously quite an effort for him and he is suffering from what is called 'perseverance' – getting 'stuck' on an action or a phrase – which affects both his actions and his speech. On the positive side, however, he can read, write (the stroke has definitely not improved his handwriting!) shave and brush his teeth himself, get his shirt on and off, and he eats his meals with virtually no assistance from me at all. Movement hasn't returned to his arm and hand.

It looks as if the planned ninety day rehab timetable is going to be drastically shortened – the physios had programmed two weeks for Freddie to be able to carry out bed to chair transfers, and he cracked it in two days! Once St Thomas's has done all it can for him, he will go to a dedicated rehabilitation centre ('The National Hospital for Neurological Disorders, in Queen's Square).

The physios have had Freddie walking with a crutch and he is doing well. The sequencing is obviously quite hard – Freddie kept veering off to the right, until the physios taped some parallel lines on the floor, so he had a target to aim at (typical Gunner or what?).

He has been given a trial in a motorised wheelchair – set to go so slowly it's almost backwards – so that his spatial abilities can be improved. At the moment, he is able to manoeuvre around obstacles but he focuses solely on them and doesn't take into account what is happening on the periphery – a bit dangerous if someone happens to be passing by, or a wall suddenly comes up to greet you…

Snookered!
The cognitive therapists seem to be working Freddie very hard – he has agreed to take part in a research programme looking at the effects of brain damage, so has sessions with psychologists as well as the 'normal' speech and language therapy (SALT) people. I sit in on the SALT meetings, and it can be quite hard at times to keep a straight face. Freddie was asked to look at some 'situation pictures' and say what was wrong; one of them showed a snooker table, with someone about to play a shot. Freddie immediately gave the SALT a critique of the player's technique and how he was addressing the cue ball totally incorrectly, where the target ball was going to go if he hit it (not in the pocket!), and how he should stand and aim if he wanted to pot the ball and return for a shot on the blue. He completely ignored the apple superimposed on the picture in the bottom left pocket…

Her Majesty is expecting me:
In all of this, Freddie is being wonderful – really co-operative, putting his all into everything asked of him and yet amazingly patient with what is being done to him. It must be so hard for someone who has been the capable and decisive person that he was to become utterly dependent but he seems to be coping with it without getting overly frustrated or angry. He is still unfailingly courteous and hospitable – therapists and doctors have now become used to Freddie offering them a cup of tea or coffee when they come to his bedside – and the 'essential Freddie' is definitely still there. I have to translate some of his expressions on occasion – for instance, when one of the doctors asked him about why he was there, Freddie told him about it being a "pretty

bad train crash". This would be immediately understandable to any of our friends but I had to explain to the doctors that it was just a phrase and yes, Freddie was totally aware of the stroke and heart surgery and didn't think that he'd been involved in an incident on the 7.20 to Waterloo! The head physio took me to one side on another occasion, rather concerned because Freddie may be hallucinating as he had told her he was meant to be at lunch with the Queen… it was Garter Day, and yes, that's where he should have been…

At Queen's (12th July 2010):
As a dedicated rehabilitation centre, Queen's is totally focussed on getting the patient to the best possible mobility and recovery – during the first week, Freddie (and I) will meet with the various therapists for detailed assessment and discussion, and they will come up with a plan based on our aspirations and their professional opinions – let's hope the two meet somewhere along the line! Their final goal is discharge to 'fulfilled living'. Freddie will be given a timetable every Friday, detailing the plans for the following week and I think he will respond very well to this planned schedule. It is going to be quite demanding for him – therapy from 8.30am until 4.30pm every weekday, with the nurses doing 'extras' during evenings and weekends but I am sure that he will benefit enormously from the focussed and concentrated rehabilitation.

St Thomas's therapists have done a really good job with Freddie and I think that it is a tribute to the physiotherapists in particular that he has been taken on at Queen's so quickly after the stroke/surgery. His physios have got Freddie walking about seventy-five metres with a crutch, able to balance sufficiently well to throw bean bags at cones (he is far too good at it!) and to stand for about five minutes (with a bar and the wheelchair handy, just in case).

Freddie's mental processes are steadily improving and I very much hope that Queen's will be able to concentrate on helping him learn how to compensate for the brain functions he has lost.

Freddie's left arm is being disappointingly non-responsive, after giving us some excitement about twitching fingers. He now has a splint to wear, as there is concern that his arm will pull across his chest and the fingers 'claw', and he may need some specialised massage and manipulation.

Two weeks in…:

I can't quite believe that nearly two weeks have passed since Freddie was transferred to Queen Square – we seem to have settled into the routines there very quickly (just hope this doesn't mean we have become thoroughly institutionalised!) There are only ten beds on this unit, so we are incredibly lucky to have been given a place. (Owing, I am sure, to the good offices of Lord Kakaar).

Freddie has been seen, talked to, analysed, prodded, poked, and generally put through his paces, and the therapists' initial impressions seem favourable. The team is working to a discharge date of 1st October, which although it seems a long time away, will come round before we know it. My goal is still to make the Regimental Reunion in Birmingham on 25th September.

I have been told to put as many different objects as I can into Freddie's left hand, as this can stimulate the brain into 'remembering' what it is like to hold things. Over the past couple of days, Freddie has been able to stretch his arm out, lift his elbow and there is slight muscle movement when he shrugs his shoulders, so something is happening.

He has been on exercise bikes to strengthen his muscles and encourage the knee to firm up – it looks very strange as his foot and hand have to be bandaged on to the pedal/handlebar to stop them slipping off – and he manages to pedal for about twenty minutes, which is fantastic.

The best thing about all this exercise is that Freddie can sense improvement, and it is such a motivator – as you can imagine, it is hard work, and he puts so much effort into it, so it is really encouraging for him to see some results. He has good banter with the physios and I think they enjoy his sense of humour and appreciate his determination.

Occupational therapists have been much more in evidence than at St Thomas's and Freddie now has the shower/shave routine down to about forty minutes with them – and he has been virtually dressing himself, apart from his left shoe and sock…

On the cognitive side, the Speech and Language chap has decided that Freddie doesn't need more than one session a week with him, and the psychologist is going to work on the 'higher cognitive processes'. She was quite positive about the possible progress Freddie could make, and they have been working through what sound like IQ tests.

We had a visit to King's last Monday for another CT scan – a routine follow up. The titanium plate (or tectonic, as Freddie calls it!) to replace the removed section of skull will not be inserted until March.

A slow and steady summer (July 2010 onwards):
There is now a more settled therapy routine, with physio every weekday as a minimum, and occupational therapy, exercise programme and a smidgeon of speech therapy and psychology thrown in for good measure! Freddie remains optimistic and generally very cheerful, although we have had a couple of 'low days'.

A walking boot has been made, which is helping his left leg take more of his weight and allowing him to walk with a (very long) stick to help his balance. He now sleeps with a splint for as many hours as he can stand it (sorry, no pun intended!) to help stretch the calf muscle. It takes him a while to find his balance but we are confident this will improve with time. Sadly, we have been advised that he will need a wheelchair for the foreseeable future, certainly for outside travel. As he still has 'left side neglect', I am a bit apprehensive about letting him loose with an electric version, as anything to his left is in severe danger of being run over! The arm is being intractable, unfortunately, and is giving him quite a lot of pain. The upper bone has dropped from the socket, although electrical stimulation (FES) does help: it is quite amazing to see the muscles being 'brought to life' and the arm being drawn up into the socket – it enables the physios to work on the shoulder and upper arm muscles without causing too much additional pain.

Freddie is still having some problems with his cognitive processes – there is some dyspraxia, which means, for instance, that I have to decipher whether he means 'today, tomorrow, or yesterday'. Processing large chunks of information is quite daunting and very tiring for him. He continues to get 'stuck' occasionally on an idea or thought but there is definitely improvement here, and it is only evident when he is tired.

A recent highlight was having the children and grandchildren to visit for lunch – we had a great day with them all and the three oldest grandchildren earned some holiday money by pushing 'Franpa's chair. Alexander (nearly 6) was very concerned to assure 'Franpa' that he was "very glad you didn't die" – out of the mouths of babes…

At ease (Autumn 2010):
I am constantly reminded of what a remarkable man I have married. Freddie never complains, and is courageous and determined in tackling the difficulties of learning to do things that we take so much for granted.

He has recently been introduced to the delights of the treadmill, both aimed at strengthening his hamstrings and knee joints to make walking less of an effort. His military background is a slight hindrance – his natural stance is with feet very close together (to attention), which means that his automatic standing position isn't very stable – until we finally hit on using 'stand at ease', which solved the problem.

I don't think we have had a day when there hasn't been at least one visitor and I am so very grateful to all of you who have managed to get in to see him.

Our big event is coming up next weekend, when we go to Dudley for the 3 RHA Past and Present Members annual get together. The Regiment has been incredibly generous, and is arranging transport for us – I was quite prepared to take the train but this will certainly make the travelling up much less stressful. I am so proud of Freddie's determination to watch the tee off at the customary golf challenge and to deliver the response speech after dinner. It will be a real milestone on this particular journey for him and I know that he will be enormously heartened by being with 'his' Regiment again.

Final update (October 26th 2010)
Now that we have been home for nearly a month, I thought you might appreciate a final update to let you know how Freddie is getting on with our new regime. I won't send out any more letters, other than to let you know how the scheduled skull reconstruction goes at the end of March. We are immensely grateful to all of you for your interest and concern and your love and prayers for Freddie and me, which have been a great comfort, not just through the initial shock of his illness, but also through the long and frustrating hospitalisation.

We have found an excellent Neuro-Physiotherapy clinic, recommended by a friend, just outside Winchester, and Freddie goes there every day for an hour. The NHS gives him an hour of physio a week, so I am very thankful that we are in a position to supplement this with private therapy. I had hoped to do rather more with Freddie at home but we are both quite tired and have had to learn to pace ourselves, so about an hour of exercise or massage is all we manage at the moment. The therapists are fantastic and are optimistic about Freddie's long-term prospects – we shall give it six months, and then reassess his needs. He is walking around the house without a stick (although I have to support from behind, in case of stumbles), navigates the various narrow inside steps, and even manages to negotiate the gravel driveway. Our Victorian house is not the easiest design for someone with mobility limitations and we have had to arrange numerous alterations to facilitate Freddie's care, such as grab rails and a wet room. The therapists are concentrating on Freddie's torso to strengthen the muscles there, which will enable him to establish his midline, resulting in better balance, which will in turn make walking easier.

Unfortunately, Freddie isn't sleeping very well at night; the stroke has affected his bladder and his brain keeps telling him he needs the loo, whether he does or not, so he wakes up between three and eight times during midnight and 6am. No wonder we are tired!

The new normal (August 2011 onwards):
Following several cancellations and a bout of MRSA, Freddie was finally admitted to King's College for the cranioplasty on 22nd August, which was 100% successful, thanks to the good work of the maxiofacial surgeon, Mr Bentley. We shall continue to travel to King's for the next three years for the heart surgeon to check that all is well but, apart from that, we are starting our 'new normal' life: not what we expected retirement to be but not what we feared it could be eighteen months ago – so the moral has to be that there is always something to be thankful for if you look hard enough!

BROWN ROD

The NHS saved my life and I will always be grateful for their expertise and support. Had I not been living in London, very close to a hospital with the ability to deal with my stroke, the outcome would have been so different. I am convinced that someone 'up there' was looking after me and that I survived for a reason.

During my recovery I had plenty of time to think, particularly at night when the wards were quiet; I dwelt a lot on my future, struggling to come to terms with the sudden and total about-face my life had taken. I loved my job in Westminster. The Lords and my other friends and comrades wrote wonderful letters to me and said they wanted me to get back to fitness and return but it became clear that this just wouldn't be possible. I felt very low at this stage but, thankfully, people who came to see me lifted my spirits a lot, particularly Lord Kakkar, Peston and Hedley Duncan, who came to see me every week, and my brilliant office girls Nic and Jo. In the months ahead, I knew that I would be responsible for planning and hosting the Queen, the US President and the Pope on their formal visits to Westminster Hall in the House of Lords to address the Lords and MPs. These were major events and I simply didn't have the physical, psychological or mental agility and capacity to produce it to the standard required. In short, I just couldn't deliver. The thought of potential failure in the face of the millions who would be watching this on TV was too much to bear – I respected the Lords too much for that. Having decided that the game was over, my focus changed to recovering as best I could, going home and being able to enjoy life with my grandchildren. I wanted to see them grow up, become good people and I resolved to do whatever I could to make that happen.

Once I was ready, I went to see the Lord Speaker, Baroness Helene Hayman, to offer my resignation. Helene was wonderfully supportive and understanding to me and to Jane (like us, she was pretty upset, too). She said that I had made the right decision and I wrote the necessary resignation letters to the House and to Buckingham Palace. My response from the Queen's Private Secretary lifted my spirits hugely; he said that he had shown the letter to the Queen. She understood, accepted my request and said that she wanted me to concentrate on recovery. That was only bettered by my private audience with Her Majesty as I paraded to 'sign off'. We spoke together for about twenty minutes, she thanked me and gave me a signed photograph of herself and Prince Philip. Lunch followed with members of her household. It was a marvellous, if sad day. I wish I could have served Her for longer but it was not to be.

My discharge in October brought its own challenges. Our house was being re-modelled in order to create a single floor bungalow to accommodate my limitations and care needs, whilst creating the space for our daughter to live above us with her two children and her husband, Jay (an ex-Sapper, we enjoy a lot of rival regimental banter). Our great friends from our days in Tidworth in the 1980s, Paddy and Annie George, brought their considerable DIY skills along to help fix things up; aids that I am still using today. We've attended the weddings of all three of their sons and it's good to stay close to them.

Following the recommendation of my late friend General Sir Christopher Wallace, I began (and still am) attending regular sessions with the physiotherapy teams. They are very experienced people and I came to enjoy being treated by the staff, who all have great experience of my condition. Every fortnight, Mark Douglas-Withers, another good friend and fellow Gunner, takes me to the treatment centre. We moan about life and generally feel better for it.

As I began to regain strength and confidence, we planned for a return to hospital to have my skull repaired with a titanium plate. I needed full-time care and Jane was marvellous throughout, as she was with looking after the stream of builders, plumbers, carpenters and decorators led by the hugely talented Mr Rob Smith who, with his wife Debs, have become good and trusted friends. Dealing with the upheaval was a very tiring time but, gradually, we got through it and my recovery continues well. I have a lot to be grateful for.

After thirty-five years' service, I don't really think about the Army at all, other than the times when I reconnect with my old Regiment (always great occasions). Jane and I attend 3 RHA's Past and Present Members Association (PPMA), which meets every year. Numbers have varied over the years but, now that the Regiment has recently returned from Germany to the UK, our attendance will continue to grow and thrive. Veterans of any age want to meet and talk about their experiences; the PPMA provides an excellent means to catch up with old friends and comrades and help those veterans who might be in need of medical, financial, psychological or other help. To enable that, former members of the Regiment, Brian O'Neill, Jeff Smith and Bob Lodge used their exceptional skill and commitment to establish a new charity called Red Cypher, which has been highly successful in supporting the serving and retired members of the Regiment. It is proof for all to see that 3 RHA looks after its own and is a wonderful initiative that continues to grow. It was my pleasure to act as the PPMA President for the sixteen years since it was first started. The reception I received on retirement was remarkable. I was replaced by David Richards, the same man who followed me as the CO, so passing on the reins as President was a particular pleasure. He is and will be a great supporter and ally.

Our Regimental gatherings are also reinforced by our attendance at the annual Remembrance Service in Whitehall. Well wrapped up in my wheelchair with Benny Benoit as my 'pusher', on a bright, chilly morning, some sixty of us gather on Horseguards and march past the Cenotaph to lay the wreath. Duty done, and with the cheers of the crowd to support us as we continue the march up the Mall and return to Horseguards, we then assemble at a nearby hotel for lunch and continue to enjoy each other's company. It reinforces the bond.

I miss the Black Rod job every day and look forward to the times when I can see my old team again and catch up with their news. It really was a very special time. Watching BBC Parliament has become an obsession!

While still serving as Adjutant General, I was invited by Dame Mary Fagan, the Lord Lieutenant of Hampshire, to become one of her Deputy Lieutenants. Mary and her husband Christopher were excellent and generous hosts during my Service and I was delighted to accept. Hampshire has a large military presence from all three Services and enjoys frequent visits by the Royal Family to one or other of our bases. My task was to stand in when the Lord Lieutenant was unavailable at various military and other important occasions. Observing Citizenship Ceremonies was an enjoyable occasion when I would witness new people from all over the world taking the oath of allegiance and congratulate them on becoming British citizens in the county of Hampshire. Meeting these people was a particular pleasure, which I was always delighted to do. Sadly, my stroke prevented me from hosting the Fagans at the State Opening of Parliament in 2010 and that remains a disappointment for me. But we are lucky to have a full and active social life, keeping up with friends old and new.

One of my most pleasurable tasks is to act as a Friend of the Memorial Chapel at Sandhurst. I appear at the chapel council meetings and services three times a year and it is a good way to keep up with events at the Academy and take friends to lunch after the service. The meal is held where I spent a year as a cadet in New College, so driving around the grounds brings back memories, good and bad.

One of my great joys in life is spending time with my grandchildren: Alex, Jemima, Isabella and Freddie. Demands of Service meant I missed a lot when Brendan and Kate were growing up, so time with those four is precious – and the healthcare professionals are convinced it's helped my cognitive recovery; children keep you on your toes and we have some great – if occasionally random – chats. They named my walking stick 'Brown Rod'. Subsequently, I have been given a new one and it's black, so it acts as a reminder of another happy time.

Post-stroke, life began to take on a familiar pattern: regular physio and sessions at the gym; occasional health check-ups; sitting on various charitable boards (although following discussions is not as easy as it used to be); rediscovering my love of riding – fostered with Sally in childhood – thanks to a local Riding for the Disabled Group, where I am a trustee. I can still swing a golf club without falling over, though admittedly I'm rarely under par these days. I enjoy keeping in touch with the members of Tidworth Garrison Golf Club. After a little over five years as the Club's President – and with my stroke telling me that it was time to step down – I was hugely honoured to be appointed a Life Member. The members are always in great humour and keep an interest in how I am faring.

I was progressing well and keeping busy when, out of the blue in May 2015, my phone rang. It was Jim Davidson OBE, whom I've known for almost twenty years. He did some great work with the Army Benevolent Fund: The Soldiers' Charity and formed a group called the British Forces Foundation, which raised money to fund entertainers so they could travel to operational locations and entertain the troops out there. Jim accompanied them and gigged in some thirteen locations, becoming devoted to the military and the Army in particular.

Jim invited us to dinner with his lovely wife, Michelle, and told us about a new venture called Care after Combat. This was another charity of which he was the Chairman, with the mission to prevent veterans in prison from re-offending through a programme of support and mentoring. Jim's enthusiasm was infectious and I told him my story about trying to launch the Veterans' Commissioner and seeing it buried by a Labour minister in the MOD. He invited me to become the charity's President. I was happy to accept and felt that I had some experience of the veteran's world and was now able to put something back into my Service. We've had some interesting adventures so far and, as I write this, Care after Combat is making a difference and Jim, Goose, Jane Jones and his supporters deserve huge credit for that. Some two years into my tenure as President, I felt that I had done all that I could to help the charity grow and develop. There was limited value in attending their fundraising events and annual Conservative party conferences and it was time to move on. But Jim remains a good friend and we laugh a lot – it helps!

Life today is not as Jane and I pictured it to be. But despite the losses, there have been gains. And I am grateful for every single one.

SO WHAT?

Looking back on my life thus far (which is not something I would recommend to everyone because I think life is for living and looking ahead), I have witnessed some major events: the end of the Cold War and its ongoing strategic impact around the world; the effects of terrorism, civil war, humanitarian disasters and political upheaval. There have been some wonderful memories too: my involvement with the Royal Family and my old Regiment, my role in the House of Lords and the people I have known there and, most importantly, my family. It has been an exciting, rewarding time. On these occasions – and thinking back at the end of this story – military men are often taught to ask: so what? It often helps to think about the outcome of any situation and discover any clues to what we should do about it.

My military career as an Army Officer began by a fortuitous exposure as a sixteen-year-old schoolboy to what life as a soldier could mean through the Combined Cadet Force (CCF). Until then, I had no idea about what I wanted to do after leaving school, other than being sure that university was not for me. I knew that I wasn't bright enough or committed enough to get the most from my undergraduate years. School prizes for achievement each summer eluded me. In fact, my first and only appearance on the podium was when I was invited back to the school as a Brigadier to present the prizes.

What I did know was that I wanted to get away from home. My parents' separation made life very difficult indeed and I missed the support from my mother and father that I should have had. It was a tense and stressful time but I found some respite in school life. Few of my teachers knew about my situation and I drifted through the days, doing the work and enjoying a sporting life. Joining the CCF then gave me a structure, programme and a way of working that appealed to me. I enjoyed the weekly training days, the inspections by our Royal Marines Instructor and camping expeditions during the school holidays. Promotion gave me new responsibilities and I thoroughly enjoyed it. Finding the recruiting brochure SANDHURST offered me what I was looking for: a two-year course with relatively easy entry qualifications, free accommodation, a salary and a Commission as an Army Officer for those who passed the course. It offered me an escape route where I could get away and start a new life on my own.

Would I recommend a military career to a young man or woman? It certainly would not suit everyone but Officer selection is a well-known and successful process that will pick out those with the potential to learn and grow as leaders. I would encourage an Army career as an excellent way to start; it will give the young officer the leadership and development skills to command soldiers often in demanding circumstances. Some officers will have opportunities to extend their terms of engagement from a short Service to a full career, provided that the individual's performance merits that. Many have served for a short time, felt that they have got what they wanted from it and moved on to a new job. That is an individual's choice and I cannot criticise it.

Although I began my Army career with a Regular

Commission, and could serve for a full career if I wanted, it and was good enough, I felt that I should keep my options open and see how things went before deciding to stay or go. As each tour of two to three years came to an end, I would think about my future and list the things that I had experienced in that time. Was what I had seen and done worth it? For the most part, I had enjoyed my time, my future appointment looked good and I decided to keep going. Marriage and children changed that thinking and our priority became bringing them up well and giving them the best possible start through a good education at a boarding school. This would provide stability and continuity for them as we might be posted out of the country and would allow them to develop strong friendships and learn good, lifelong values. That was an expensive exercise in itself, despite the allowances we received but, as parents, we thought it was the best we could do. It was a struggle but the result has produced two great people. Eventually, I reached the stage in my personal assessment where I felt that I had been promoted at the right time, had been offered good jobs, was enjoying my time and should keep going to see how far my career could go. I have no complaints.

The majority of my career has been involved in facing down the thug and the bully – the IRA, the slaughter of the innocents in Bosnia, and the oppression in Iraq. The time during and after the Cold War and subsequent events around the world created a tension that causes people to feel insecure and uncertain. We all know that there is much that is not right in the world and many of us think that we know the solutions to put things right. It is a fact that life is more complicated than that and history is littered with examples of individuals, nations and organisations that have got things spectacularly wrong. Keeping any country secure in its own borders and abroad is the greatest and most demanding responsibility for any government and we have to deal with life as it is, not as we would wish it to be. Making the change takes time and requires a great deal of thought and determination to see it to a successful outcome. The answer does not lie in arrogance and complacency if we are to influence the thinking of those in power at the time. It requires humility, judgement and honesty, backed up by the strength of character and capability to see it through. People who do not have these qualities should be treated with real caution – they are dangerous.

My life as an Army Officer has brought its rewards, experiences and life lessons. I have observed my senior leaders and commanders at close quarters and tried to follow their example. Equally, I have seen other men whom I would not wish to copy. I have seen how their methods and actions have caused a lot of distress through their ambition and lack of respect for the effect on their subordinates, who are good people with real merit able to offer genuine value. Too often, I have heard the phrase, "That's just x, you know what he's like." But that is to excuse and it fails to correct bad leadership. If our Army is to have real utility in the future, we need to do all we can to stop the kind of behaviour that results in badly-led men and women. It represents a risk to our reputation.

My experiences of working in the Ministry of Defence in a variety of appointments have affected my views of working within the military and the national political scene. Life is a cyclical affair and I've seen the actions of successive parties in power. As far as the financial challenge is concerned, the last fifty years have seen societal demands and expectations for betterment grow with ever increasing demands on the Government's Budget. Conservatives come to power and Defence Ministers screw down on defence spending to 'make savings' – the cute way to describe cuts and efficiencies. Labour arrives and often relaxes the pressure. In the competition for resources, launching Defence Reviews is a common activity. They are described in different ways to conceal the effects but these reviews generally lead to reductions. The often mis-quoted Parkinson's Law applies: when life gets difficult and there are no easy answers, start a study and present an illusion of positive progress. The outcome is usually a loss of military capability when those in authority underplay the outcome, claiming that 'more is being done for less', that technology replaces the ability to produce the desired result and that our country's commitment to the defence effort is undimmed. These are hollow words to me and ignore the reality. When former senior and experienced officers express their concern, too often I hear successive Secretaries of State, prompted no doubt by their media advisors, reply: "Well, he is retired, so he would say that wouldn't he?" But what if they are right? What if operational effectiveness is being undermined? I watch with growing concern as the nation's military capability has declined in scale and effect since the 1940s and I hope that, when called to arms to combat a clear threat to our national security, we are not found wanting. It will be too late by then and the siren voices of the retired community will be forgotten. Society certainly won't be reminded of it. Who will be held to account? The media should retain these interviews and be ready to show them again.

Is there a solution? There is, but it won't be cheap. If we wish to play our part in maintaining global security – and I believe we should – then we will have to pay to sustain the transatlantic UK-US partnership, our independent nuclear deterrent, and maintain well-trained and equipped Force levels capable of contributing to crises around the world. Sustaining these levels over time requires a realistic assessment of the commitment required. Just think how long our engagement lasted in Northern Ireland, the Balkans, Iraq and Afghanistan. Go fast, go early and get back is not realistic and ignores the financial implications. As General Sir Rupert Smith once wisely said: *Putting the arm in the mangle is easy. Getting it out again is a bit more difficult.* Our allocation for defence from the nations' Gross Domestic Product must be seen as the bare minimum and it is reasonable to see it grow, year on year.

Historically, our experience of dealing with the media has made the military nervous of talking to journalists and commentators for fear of leaking unwelcome news or contradicting Government policy. The Civil Service in the MOD has played its part here. Some would say they try to avoid being interviewed and don't like to be seen and heard but secretly relish the chance to be on show. I did not welcome doing so but I had undergone media training before my appointment as a brigadier and been trained to appear live and recorded on camera and via the radio in a variety of benign or aggressive scenarios. I learned the importance of preparing for these sessions and always having the answers ready in case I was door-stepped at any time. I had appeared on a variety of programmes about the military, on and off operations, and been interviewed by most of the well-known commentators. These had gone well enough and I was able to satisfy the Army, the MOD and the families affected. Only one, a Labour MP, was sufficiently upset that he went for me and tried to undermine my credibility as AG. Ten years on, evidence has shown that he was wrong and he has still not apologised. I hope he understands that I would be the first to praise the MOD's work on military accommodation if it was deserved. It wasn't, so he could expect nothing less.

The incident with the MP aside, the coverage I received by the media as AG was generally fair and balanced. Occasionally, a well-known and respected journalist would ring me to ask if a particular story was worth pursuing. If I said no, he would usually let it go but, if I thought that something needed to be covered, I would give him the background and the key issues and a useful soundbite to include. Promoting the benefits of resourcing the Military Covenant proved to be really helpful.

My time as AG gave me immense pride in the soldiers and families and I witnessed their actions with great satisfaction, despite what was being asked of them. Occasionally, they did things that I would find completely unhelpful and unnecessary without a good explanation. We dealt with the miscreants, listened to any appeals they had and tried to be as reasonable as possible. Too often, we found that the issue revolved around poor leadership by individuals who did not understand their people or take the time to get to know them.

As far as my own leaders are concerned, there are those who have inspired me along the way; I have seen and learned from a host of great men and commanders of real ability.

Peter Bonnet, my first real Battery Commander, was a man I respected and from whom I learned a great deal as a young officer. He once said to me that, whatever I was doing, I should ask myself, "Am I proud of that?" There will always be, he said, something that can be done better – but do your best in the time available.

That was reinforced by the advice I received from Mr Michael Hockney, an experienced management consultant. As he and I were developing the Army's Human Resources Strategy in the mid-1990s, he encouraged me to always look at what he called 'The Machinery' – the structures and organisation in place to make things happen. I can think of a number of examples at home and abroad where the machinery was patently wrong and we struggled to work our way through it.

I count myself very fortunate indeed to have worked closely with General Sir Mike Jackson in a variety of command and Staff appointments. Jacko's judgement and ability to see the key to a particular issue was uncanny. I learned a lot from him and there were times when I got it wrong. I'm sure I tested his patience but he trusted me and let me deal with it. In his various roles, he would encourage me to always focus on the 'Ends, Ways and Means' when trying to resolve a particular difficulty. It has come to my aid on a number of occasions.

Richard, now Lord Dannatt and former head of the Army, whose remarkable career is recorded in his autobiography *Leading from the Front,* provided me with a great deal of encouragement and support at a very testing time. He gave me the direction I needed to carry on, particularly as we strove to develop the nation's understanding of the Military Covenant and the need to improve the lot of the veteran. He will always be a friend to Jane and me.

Finally, Major General Andrew Ritchie has provided what I think is the best example of how to live a fulfilled and rewarding life. Andrew is an old ally from our time in 3 RHA and we have served together in a number of different guises. During his time as the Army's Personnel Director, Andrew devised a code that serves us well. It's called the Army's Core Values and there are six of them:

* Loyalty
* Integrity
* Courage
* Discipline
* Respect for Others
* Selfless Commitment

It's not a bad model for life.

I'm not sure my courage has ever really been tested, although I am comfortable with taking risks and have done, on several occasions. As for the other five values, I am happy to be judged on what I have done and what I am.

2018
Hampshire

Head: Following my stroke and prior to my cranioplasty operation (insertion of titanium plate to replace skull bone that had to be removed)
Hampshire, 2011

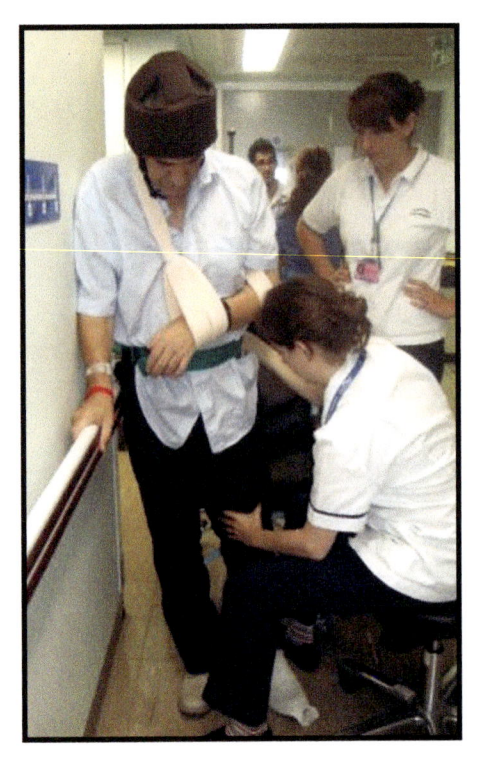

First Walk: At St Thomas' Hospital walking for the first time following the stroke
London, 2010

Brown Rod: Back on my feet at home with "brown rod"
Hampshire, 2012

RDA: 'Still riding! Felt good to get back on horseback, riding Molly with our local Riding for the Disabled. Preparing to trot, I'm still backward leaning
Tidworth, 2015

3RHA Reunion: With my fellow ex-commanding officers of 3RHA at the annual Officers' Reunion
Larkhill, 2012

My brilliant physio team without whose support and expertise I would be a lot less steady on my feet today. I've been in their care for eight years, having started my treatment in 2010 upon discharge from hospital
Winchester, 2018

Enham: Opening the café at Enham Trust, a charity for disabled people, of which I was Trustee from 2012-2015
Hampshire, 2018

Jim Davidson OBE, founder of Care After Combat, the charity of which I was President 2014-2017
Portsmouth, 2015

With the family in the garden at our home in Hampshire, 2018

APPENDIX 1 – CV

29 Jun 1951	Born Yelverton, near Tavistock Devon.
Education 1955-1961	Gulworthy School Milton Abbott Devon, Coram's Lane and Beech Grove School Wellington Somerset.
Education 1961-1969	Wellington School Somerset.
1969-1972	Royal Military Academy Sandhurst.
14 April 1972	Commissioned into the Royal Regiment of Artillery as a second lieutenant.
April-September 1972	Young Officers' Course, Larkhill Wiltshire.
September 1972	Posted to 40 Field Regiment Royal Artillery Gutersloh West Germany.
Apr-Jul 1973	Ireland Tour, Londonderry and Belfast.
14 July 1973	Marriage to Jane.
14 October 1973	Promoted to Lieutenant.
July 1975	Posted to Junior Leaders Regiment, Bramcote Nuneaton.
September 1975	Son Brendan born.

1977/8	Ireland Tour, Belfast.
September 1977	Posted to 3rd Regiment Royal Horse Artillery Devizes, then Paderborn.
14 April 1978	Promoted to Captain.
Spetember1978	Daughter, Katherine, born.
December 1980	Posted to MOD, London.
October 1982-83	Posted to Shrivenham – Staff College.
September 1983	Promoted to Major.
December 1983	Battery Commanders' course – posted to command J Battery 3rd Regiment.
December 1985	Posted to 1 Infantry Brigade as Chief of Staff, Tidworth.
1988	Appointed MBE in NY Honours.
30 June 1988	Promoted to Lieutenant Colonel.
1988	Directing Staff at Staff College, Camberley.
1989	Lieutenant Colonel Command appointment, 3 RHA Paderborn.
1990	Regiment moves from Paderborn to Colchester, joining 19th Infantry Brigade.
20 June 1992	Promoted to Colonel.
1992	MOD – Central Staff Directorate of Defence Policy.
1993	MOD – Defence Costs Study.
30 Dec 1994	Promoted to Brigadier.
Jan 1995	Higher Command and Staff course, Camberley.
Jan 1995	Commander Royal Artillery HQ 3rd Division, Bulford.

APPENDIX 2 – IRAQ INQUIRY

1995	Bosnia Herzegovina as part of NATO Implementation Force (IFOR).
1997	Director of Manning (Army), Upavon. 24 March 1999 Bosnia as Commander Multinational Division (South-West) in NATO Stabilisation Force (SFOR).
November 2000	Awarded Queen's Commendation for Valuable Service for work in Bosnia.
9 February 2000 – May 2003	Chief of Staff, Headquarters Land Command, Wilton.
11 May 2000	Appointed Deputy Colonel Commandant of the Adjutant General's Corps.
May 2003	Appointed Senior British Military Representative and Deputy Commanding General, Multinational Force, Iraq, based in Baghdad following its occupation by US and British forces.
April 2004	Appointed a Companion of the Order of St Michael and St George (CMG) for Service in Iraq October 2003.
October 2003	Appointed Military Secretary (MS) and Chief Executive Army Personnel Centre, Glasgow.
April 2005	Promoted to Lieutenant General and appointed Adjutant General, Upavon.
July 2005	Appointed Colonel Commandant Royal Regiment of Artillery.

3 November 2003	Appointed Colonel Commandant Adjutant General's Corps.
2007	Appointed a Knight Commander of the Order of the Bath (KCB) in the New Year's Honours List.
June 2008	Appointed a Deputy Lieutenant of Hampshire in June 2008.
October 2008	Retired from Army.
December 2008	Announcement made – appointed to House of Lords as Black Rod.
April 2009	Took up appointment as Black Rod.
December 2009	Gave evidence to Iraq Inquiry chaired by Sir John Chilcott.
May 2010	Stroke.
October 2010	Resigned because of ill health.

APPENDIX 2 – IRAQ INQUIRY

Records of the evidence I gave at the Iraq Inquiry can be found at www.iraqinquiry.org and extracts are reproduced here.

The notes provided below were written by Lieutenant General Sir Freddie Viggers in preparation for his hearing and submitted to the Iraq Inquiry on 8th December 2009. These notes were referred to during the hearing on 9th December 2009 and Lieutenant General Sir Freddie Viggers indicated that he was content for these notes to be made public.

The headings used for the notes below reflect those given to the witness prior to the hearing as an indication of the matters which the Inquiry wishes to cover during the session. This is detailed in paragraph seven of the Witness Protocol.

Where abbreviations were made in the original notes; these have been expanded.

Your Role
Notice of and preparation for your posting to Iraq:
I was warned off in April 2003 to fill a new post in the emerging senior coalition military command structure in the Coalition Provisional Authority (CPA) Baghdad, to start work in May. I arrived in the CPA shortly after the arrival of Coalition Forces in Baghdad, post the invasion and as the Reconstruction phase was beginning.

I acted as the 2* (Major General) Deputy Commander to the 3* Commander of Combined Joint Task Force-7 (CJTF-7), Lt Gen Sanchez. He assumed the role after the departure of Lt Gens McKiernan (who had commanded the Land Force Component during the invasion) and Lt Gen Wallace (Commander of the US V Corps).

Your role in Baghdad:
I acted as the senior British Military Representative in Iraq (SBMR-I) and as the Deputy Commander CJTF-7. My focus was on the military aspects of the reconstruction plan being delivered by the CPA. Initially, I worked from the US military HQ based at Baghdad Airport and, eventually, I was based in Green Zone once we had found a secure UK base there. My task was to provide the link between military HQ in the CPA and the heads of various civil functions in the CPA. There was a separate Deputy Commander for Operations in the CJTF-7 HQ – Major General Wadjikowski – who was based in Corps HQ at the Airport.

I provided military advice and information to the British Ambassadors, primarily to John Sawers inside the CPA. I also liaised with Ambassador Chris Segar who was based at the British Embassy in Baghdad but outside the Green Zone. Later (much later and too late), I advised and supported Ambassadors Sir Jeremy Greenstock and Sir Hilary Synnott.

I was the national focus for the expanding British military presence in Baghdad. This started at about fifteen personnel, and increased during my time to about a hundred. I did not command the troops of the British Division in Multinational Division South East (MND(SE)).

I also carried out a limited liaison function with the UN HQ and other NGOs in Baghdad, particularly the International Committee of the Red Cross (ICRC).

LINES OF REPORTING –
TO THE COALITION AND TO THE UK
Coalition:
I had daily meetings and discussions with Gen Sanchez and his senior staff (Chief of Staff Brigadier Haan), the Deputy Commander Operations, the Political Adviser and senior staff officers). I attended the daily 06:30 morning briefs and numerous planning meetings through the days and weeks.

I attended Ambassador Bremer's daily 07:00 morning briefs with Gen Sanchez and various planning meetings particularly those affecting security. I worked closely with Ambassador Bremer's Chief of Staff (Kennedy) and his Principal Adviser (McMannaway) and with the key players involved in security functions (especially Walt Slocomb (responsible for building the new Iraqi Army) and with Bernard Kerik (responsible for building the Iraqi police)).

Later, I had close contact with Andy Bearpark on the coordination of planning on reconstruction initiatives in the CPA (e.g. power generation and distribution; currency exchange); and with Deputy Chief Constable Doug Brand (seconded from the South Yorkshire Police Force and working with Kerik).

I began weekly meetings with senior UN figures, including De Mello (killed in VBIED attack on UN HQ) and his Deputy.

My dealings with the ICRC took place every three weeks or so.

UK:
I reported direct to the Chief of Defence Staff (CDS) in the MOD and to Chief of Joint Operations (CJO) in the Permanent Joint HQ (PJHQ) in Northwood. I also dealt closely in the MOD with the Deputy Chief of Defence Staff (Commitments) (Lt Gen Pigott, then Lt Gen Fry).

I maintained daily contact with the GOC (MND(SE)) or his Chief of Staff.

I submitted twice weekly reports to MOD in time for video conferences and Chiefs of Staff meetings, reporting on CPA-wide issues, not just military activity or events in MND(SE). These were sent direct to CDS and CJO, copied to MND(SE) and the British Military representative in the US CENTCOM HQ in Tampa.

Frequent liaison with CJO and his staff in PJHQ and with the MOD Iraq Policy Unit was carried out by phone, weekly video conferences and visits.

I had daily meetings with Ambassador Sawers and Greenstock and met approximately weekly with Ambassador Segar.

I submitted an end of tour report on return to UK in September.

Your relationship with the Senior British Civilian in Iraq, the British military in the South, the CPA and the UN
See above.

THE OVERALL CAMPAIGN PLAN AND THE UK'S ROLE AND CONTRIBUTION:
There was no Coalition civil-military plan for the post-invasion phase; there was no work up of the CPA staffs prior to deployment. UK elements in CPA deployed incrementally over first five months (as did other nations' contributions). CPA was never fully staffed in my time.

The overall civil-military Campaign Plan developed as experience and exposure to the scale and realities of the task emerged. Military aspects of the overall plan – primarily about security and building Iraqi Army/security forces – were developed under Gen Abizaid (Commander CENTCOM) and Gen Sanchez but we were not able to synchronise this fully with civilian aspects (governance, reconstruction, the economy, medical, education etc) until much later.

We lacked clear statements from Capitals on Coalition political-military objectives, timelines, what the end state should look like or how we were to get there. At the outset, we had no clearly stated definition of what "success" would look like for the Iraqis, the region or the international community. So we suffered from lack of clarity about Ends, Ways and Means. The Plan emerged piecemeal and was prone to dislocation by breaking news and by events.

At the outset, the CPA had no machinery or processes to turn policy decisions into coordinated delivery at national level and in the regions. CPA was disjointed, stove-piped and reactive. This improved over the first few months as the different elements of the CPA became familiar with combined working.

This was exacerbated by confused lines of responsibility between the CPA and other key players, eg Office of Reconstruction and Humanitarian Assistance (ORHA) (until it left), and by lack of contact with the UN and other NGOs.

Planning in London was too focussed on events in Basra

and MND(SE) and did not appreciate the importance of full coordination with broader Coalition plans for the rest of country; e.g. oil, power distribution, Shia communities in Basra and in Baghdad (Sadr city).

YOUR STRATEGY AND OBJECTIVES:
* To establish the UK presence and role in the CJTF-7 military command structure.
* To provide a positive contribution in CPA and CJTF-7 planning and activities.
* To report developments across the spectrum of CPA activity.
* To identify how/where the British contribution could be best focussed as required.
* To inform and alert UK on the CPA's developing plans and intentions.
* To ensure that British elements outside MND(SE) had the wherewithal to execute their roles and tasks.

THE UK'S RESPONSIBILITIES AS AN "OCCUPYING POWER"
A question for FCO, MOD and the lawyers.

INTERACTIONS WITH THE US:
These grew in effect as personalities became familiar with working together in a civilian-military structure.

Some of the civilian agencies inside the CPA were suspicious of, and did not see /understand how the military could contribute. Reluctant to engage in detailed planning prior to launching a task.

APPENDIX 2 – IRAQ INQUIRY

Priorities (e.g. security, reconstruction, finding WMD) and how those were decided:

Everything was a priority – security, the rebuild, creating the political architecture, capture Saddam, stop the sabotage and smuggling, sustain flows of vital supplies to nation, get the economy going, remove the weapons (tons, of all types).

Security was the overriding and increasingly difficult task – understand the linkages and pressures; secure and improve the infrastructure; understand and deal with the effects of internal and external influences; deal with the lack of security architecture – no Iraqi Army, police, judges, courts, jails, border controls, communications.

The military contribution to reconstruction was vital – coordination with the civilian agencies inside the CPA, and with Contractors had not been thought through at the outset.

I was not involved in the WMD issue, other than coordinating support to Iraq Survey Group activities when requested.

Impact of media and public opinion:

There was a complete failure to establish a coherent information campaign.

There was inadequate analysis of Arab media outlets or a coherent plan to get the facts onto the street (Arab and in capitals).

The situation in Iraq:

Your understanding, at the time, of the political and security situation on the ground when you arrived:

The Coalition failed to appreciate (or find out about) the state of the country, prior to the invasion: the effects of UN sanctions, fear of Saddam and the Ba'athist regime; broken infrastructure, impatience, revenge, inadequate life support, poor/non-existent communications, access to weapons, conflicting internal and external international and regional agendas.

The Coalition failed to understand the dynamics of the country – Shia/Sunni/Kurd tensions and malevolent influences inside the country and the region; or to exploit the potential benefits that could be achieved through other influencers, especially the Sheiks.

Capitals were slow to realise that it was not "job done" but "job just started". The post-invasion honeymoon was very short lived, and measured in days. It took too long for Capitals to get it.

The CPA was trying to achieve multiple and un-sequenced missions, all at the same time: build itself; try to run the country day to day; kick start the economy; deliver "democracy"; maintain security within the country and along its borders; deal with increasing terrorist and criminal activity; create confidence in the international effort among Iraqi organisations and on the street. Iraqis were impatient and suspicious, e.g. where was the oil revenue going?

The CPA was understaffed by quality and quantity.

There was an unwillingness in Capitals to take forward the mission with urgency, e.g. poor follow through of requests to act/provide.

In London, there were too many lines of reporting and accountability: Cabinet-FCO-MOD-DFID. No single Minister in charge.

Incoherent policy making and decisions, e.g. disbanding what was left of the Army and not paying the excluded military; removing the top four layers of the Ba'athist party with no alternative sources of leadership/management (left highest Iraqi military rank as major).

The long screwdriver from Washington, e.g. Rumsfeld's stream of orders and instructions and unwieldy budgetary controls.

The way in which that developed during your time in Iraq and the implications for the military.

Slow and halting reactions, e.g. manning the Governorate teams; releasing the money for local projects. Security forces took the brunt of Iraqi impatience and frustration.

Too many tasks were laid on the military without the resources or authority to deliver: security, training and mentoring, governance, law and order.

SECURITY SITUATION IN MND(SE):
For the GOCs MND(SE) to advise.

ROLE OF THE IRAQI SECURITY FORCES AND BUILDING THEIR CAPABILITY:
For others to advise.

CONCLUSIONS AND RECOMMENDATIONS.
First six months post invasion showed:
* No Campaign Plan to link the various lines of civil-military activity from the outset.
* Complete lack of cultural and environmental awareness of the country in coalition Capitals and in the CPA.
* Failure to appreciate how long the task would take, or the right road to travel.
* Need to train and prepare for the aftermath harder than training for the invasion.
* Lack of clear lines of political-military responsibility and accountability in and between capitals.
* Poor linkage between policy decision making and delivery on the ground.
* Lack of a coherent Information Campaign inside the country and internationally.

DFID was a serious bar to progress. This should not be a separate autonomous department of government. It should be an agent of the FCO, as it was (when called the Overseas Development Agency (ODA) during the Bosnia campaign.

We have to work out how better to deploy and use the non-kinetic arsenal: money, information, facilities, machinery, and expertise.

We need more and better education and training of officials in capitals who have a role in directing the political and political-military aspects of the Strategy in this kind of Campaign. This must include Ministers and senior civil servants. It is not a job for amateurs. We must make more and better use of non-governmental expertise and agencies in planning and directing the Campaign.

Planning and decision-taking in Capitals needs to match the tempo of events and the pace of life on the ground.